At Issue

How Should Obesity
Be Treated?

Other Books in the At Issue Series:

At Issue

How Should Obesity Be Treated?

Stefan Kiesbye, Book Editor

GREENHAVEN PRESS
A part of Gale, Cengage Learning

GALE
CENGAGE Learning™

Detroit • New York • San Francisco • New Haven, Conn • Waterville, Maine • London

GALE
CENGAGE Learning

Christine Nasso, *Publisher*
Elizabeth Des Chenes, *Managing Editor*

For more information, contact:
Greenhaven Press
27500 Drake Rd.
Farmington Hills, MI 48331-3535
Or you can visit our Internet site at gale.cengage.com

Articles in Greenhaven Press anthologies are often edited for length to meet page requirements. In addition, original titles of these works are changed to clearly present the main thesis and to explicitly indicate the author's opinion. Every effort is made to ensure that Greenhaven Press accurately reflects the original intent of the authors. Every effort has been made to trace the owners of copyrighted material.

Cover image © Images.com/Corbis.

LIBRARY OF CONGRESS CATALOGING-IN-PUBLICATION DATA

How should obesity be treated? / Stefan Kiesbye, book editor.
   p. cm. -- (At issue)
Includes bibliographical references and index.
ISBN 978-0-7377-4422-4 (hardcover)
ISBN 978-0-7377-4423-1 (pbk.)
1. Obesity--Popular works. I. Kiesbye, Stefan.
RC628.H69 2009
616.3'98--dc22

                                            2009013595

Contents

Introduction

Responding to a 911 call in August 2004, paramedics arrived at Gayle Laverne Grinds's duplex in Martin County, Florida. The *Palm Beach Post* reports on what they found: "She lived in filth, so large she couldn't move from her sofa, even to use the bathroom. Early Wednesday, still fused to the couch, Gayle Laverne Grinds died following a six-hour effort by rescue workers who struggled to lift the 480-pound woman and get her to a Martin County hospital. Unable to separate the skin of the 39-year-old woman from her sofa, 12 Martin County Fire-Rescue workers slid both onto a trailer and hauled her behind a pickup to Martin Memorial Hospital South. She died a short time later."

During the rescue efforts, the scenes inside and outside Grinds's duplex turned absurd. According to the *Palm Beach Post*, "Workers wore protective clothing and installed large air handling hoses to ventilate the horrendous odor coming from the home while trying to figure out how to get the woman and her couch to the hospital. The street in front of the row of duplex apartments turned into a makeshift construction site as rescue crews used hammers and chain saws to build a large wooden stretcher with handles cut around the perimeter so firefighters could lift the woman and the couch."

Although this story presents an extreme example, obesity has become a significant health concern. Obesity in America and around the world is on the rise. The Weight-Control Information Network, an information service of the National Institute for Diabetes and Digestive and Kidney Diseases (NIDDK) reports that 66 percent of all adults age 20 and older are overweight, and 31.4 percent are obese. Only 32.3 percent of all adults are considered to be at a healthy weight. The NIDDK states that, "The prevalence [of obesity and overweight] has steadily increased over the years among both gen-

ders, all ages, all racial and ethnic groups, all educational levels, and all smoking levels. From 1960 to 2004, the prevalence
of overweight increased from 44.8 to 66 percent in U.S. adults
age 20 to 74. The prevalence of obesity during this same time
period more than doubled among adults age 20 to 74 from
13.3 to 32.1 percent, with most of this rise occurring since
1980."

Being overweight or obese might not always have immedi-
ate consequences for one's health, and does not necessarily
lead to a gruesome death, but the NIDDK warns that "Most
studies show an increase in mortality rates associated with
obesity. Individuals who are obese have a 10- to 50-percent
increased risk of death from all causes, compared with healthy
weight individuals." In America, about 112,000 excess deaths
per year occur relative to people who maintain a healthy
weight. Cardiovascular causes are mostly to blame.

Perhaps most alarming is that obesity is becoming more
prevalent in children and adolescents. According to the
NIDDK, "While there is no generally accepted definition for
obesity as distinct from *overweight* in children and adolescents,
the prevalence of overweight is increasing for children and
adolescents in the United States. Approximately 17.5 percent
of children (age 6 to 11) and 17 percent of adolescents (age
12 to 19) were overweight in 2001 to 2004."

At a recent conference of the American Heart Association,
a number of studies revealed that many obese and overweight
young children had arteries similar to 45-year-olds, as well as
heart abnormalities that increased the risk of heart disease.
Dr. Travis Stork, host of the television show *The Doctors*, said
in an interview that "In the world of medicine, there's a saying: 'You're only as young as your oldest part.' This is going to
lead to strokes, heart attacks. This is probably going to take 5,
10, 15, 20 years off these kids' lives."

But overweight and obese children are not only at risk of
losing years of their life through illness. Obesity also increases

the risk for severe emotional problems, mental disorders, and depression. According to the American Psychiatric Association (APA), "A study at the University of Medicine and Dentistry of New Jersey found that obese girls ages 13 to 14 are four times more likely to experience low self-esteem than non-obese girls. The study also reported that obese boys and girls with low self-esteem had higher rates of loneliness, sadness, and nervousness. These children were more likely to smoke and drink alcohol compared with obese children with normal self-esteem. Depression, often an outcome of low self-esteem, affects as many as 750,000 teens in the U.S."

Depression can also be an effect of obesity. If children are teased about their weight, they develop symptoms of depression. In 2006, Megan Meier, a 13-year-old girl who had struggled with her weight, was contacted by 16-year-old Josh Evans via MySpace. Megan was battling low self-esteem and depression and was flattered by the boy's attention. After befriending Megan, Josh turned hostile, calling Megan "fat" and a "slut." He told her that "the world would be a better place without her." Devastated by Josh's maliciousness, Megan committed suicide.

The case became notorious largely because Josh Evans turned out to be a fabrication by an adult female neighbor, who took part in a scheme of revenge on Megan for allegedly badmouthing her daughter. But Megan's story is also noteworthy for the harmful psychological effects that obesity and a negative body image can have on teenagers. According to the APA, a University of Minnesota study "reveals that children who were teased about being overweight were more likely to have poor body image, low self-esteem, and symptoms of depression. The study found that 26 percent of teens who were teased at school and home reported they had considered suicide, and 9 percent had attempted it. Suicide is the third leading cause of death among adolescents."

Obesity is a complex problem. While obese and overweight people are often stigmatized as a result of cultural misconceptions about their physical condition, medical research has begun to reveal that in addition to poor diet and exercise, genetic, behavioral, and environmental factors may also contribute to obesity. The diversity of opinions expressed in *At Issue: How Should Obesity Be Treated?* demonstrates that there is no consensus or simple solution to what is becoming a significant public health issue in the United States and around the world.

Medications Can Promote Weight Loss

Weight-Control Information Network

The Weight-Control Information Network is an information service of the National Institute of Diabetes and Digestive and Kidney Diseases (NIDDK).

Obesity is a widespread medical condition that affects millions of people. While changing eating and exercise habits is the preferred method for reducing one's weight, prescription weight-loss medications might be a solution for patients whose increased weight puts them at medical risk. The long-term safety of prescription drugs on the market is largely untested, and these medications can come with side effects. Most medications are only approved for short-term use, and their effectiveness can vary widely in patients. However, patients have to be aware that potential abuse, dependence, and development of tolerance are risks involved in taking weight-loss medications and that drugs are not meant to act as a substitute for maintaining a healthy lifestyle.

Obesity is a chronic disease that affects many people. To lose weight and maintain weight loss over the long term, it is necessary to modify one's diet and engage in regular physical activity. Some people, however, may require additional treatment. As with other chronic conditions, such as diabetes or high blood pressure, the use of prescription medications may be appropriate for some people who are overweight or obese.

Weight-Control Information Network, "Prescription Medications for the Treatment of Obesity," Weight-Control Information Network, December 2007. Reproduced by permission.

Prescription weight-loss medications should be used only by patients who are at increased medical risk because of their weight. They should not be used for "cosmetic" weight loss. In addition, patients should have previously tried to lose weight through diet and physical activity.

Prescription weight-loss drugs are approved only for those with:

- A body mass index (BMI) of 30 and above.

- A BMI of 27 and above with an obesity-related condition, such as high blood pressure, type 2 diabetes, or dyslipidemia (abnormal amounts of fat in the blood).

BMI is a measure of weight in relation to height that helps determine if your weight places your health at risk. A BMI of 18.5 to 24.9 is considered healthy. A BMI of 25 to 30 is considered overweight, and a BMI over 30 is considered obese. . . .

Although most side effects of prescription medications for obesity are mild, serious complications have been reported. Also, few studies have evaluated the long-term safety or effectiveness of weight-loss medications. Weight-loss medications should *always* be combined with a program of healthy eating and regular physical activity. . . .

Food and Drug Administration–Approved Prescription Weight-Loss Medications

Most of the Food and Drug Administration (FDA)–approved weight-loss medications are approved for short-term use, meaning a few weeks, but doctors may prescribe them for longer periods of time—a practice called "off-label" use. . . . Sibutramine and orlistat are the only weight-loss medications approved for longer-term use in patients who are significantly obese. Their safety and effectiveness have not been established for use beyond 2 years, however.

Appetite Suppressants. Most available weight-loss medications approved by the FDA are appetite-suppressant medications. These include sibutramine, phentermine, phendimetrazine, and diethylpropion. Appetite-suppressant medications promote weight loss by decreasing appetite or increasing the feeling of being full. These medications make you feel less hungry by increasing one or more brain chemicals that affect mood and appetite. Phentermine and sibutramine are the most commonly prescribed appetite-suppressants in the United States. . . .

Lipase Inhibitors. The drug orlistat reduces the body's ability to absorb dietary fat by about one-third. It does this by blocking the enzyme lipase, which is responsible for breaking down dietary fat. When fat is not broken down, the body cannot absorb it, so it is eliminated and fewer calories are taken in.

In early 2007, orlistat was approved for over-the-counter (OTC) sale for adults age 18 and over. This means that the drug may be purchased without a prescription. The OTC version of orlistat is sold under the brand name alli. Alli is meant to be taken with a reduced-calorie, low-fat diet, exercise, and a daily multivitamin. Its side effects are similar to those for prescription orlistat. . . .

Other Medications

The following types of medication are not FDA-approved for the treatment of obesity. However, they have been shown to promote short-term weight loss in clinical studies and may be prescribed off-label.

Drugs to treat depression. Some antidepressant medications have been studied as appetite-suppressant medications. While these medications are FDA-approved for the treatment of depression, their use in weight loss is an off-label use. . . . Studies of these medications have generally found that patients lose modest amounts of weight for up to 6 months, but that patients tend to regain weight while they are still on the drug. One exception is bupropion. In one study, patients taking bupropion maintained weight loss for up to 1 year.

Drugs to treat seizures. Two medications used to treat seizures, topiramate and zonisamide, have been shown to cause weight loss. Whether these drugs will be useful in treating obesity is being studied.

Drugs to treat diabetes. The diabetes medication metformin may promote small amounts of weight loss in people with obesity and type 2 diabetes. How this medication promotes weight loss is not clear, although research has shown reduced hunger and food intake in people taking the drug.

Drug combinations. The combined drug treatment using fenfluramine and phentermine (known as "fen/phen") is no longer available due to the withdrawal of fenfluramine from the market after some patients experienced serious heart and lung disorders. . . . Little information is available about the safety or effectiveness of other drug combinations for weight loss, including fluoxetine/phentermine, phendimetrazine/phentermine, orlistat/sibutramine, herbal combinations, or others. . . .

Research has yet to determine the long-term health effects of weight-loss drugs.

Drugs in development. Many medications are being tested as potential treatments for obesity. The makers of one drug, rimonabant, applied for FDA approval in 2007 but withdrew the application after a scientific panel recommended against the drug's use. Although rimonabant is approved for use in some countries, it is *not* approved for use in the United States.

Weight Loss Responses Can Differ

People respond differently to weight-loss medications, and some people experience more weight loss than others. Weight-loss medications lead to an average weight loss of about 10 pounds more than what you might lose with nondrug obesity treatments. Maximum weight loss usually occurs within 6 months of starting the medicine. Weight then tends to level off or increase during the remainder of treatment.

Over the short term, weight loss in individuals who are obese may reduce a number of health risks. Studies have found that weight loss with some medications improves blood pressure, blood cholesterol, triglycerides (fats), and insulin resistance (the body's inability to use blood sugar). New research suggests that long-term use of weight-loss medications may help individuals keep off the weight they have lost. However, more studies are needed to determine the long-term effects of weight-loss medications on weight and health.

Research has yet to determine the long-term health effects of weight-loss drugs. To date, the longest study is a 4-year investigation of orlistat. Most other studies have lasted 6 to 12 months or less. In addition, research has not examined rare side effects (those occurring in less than 1 per 1,000 patients), and the optimal duration of treatment is unknown.

When considering long-term weight-loss drugs to treat obesity, you should consider the following areas of concern and potential risks.

Potential for abuse or dependence. Currently, all prescription medications to treat obesity except orlistat are controlled substances, meaning doctors need to follow certain restrictions when prescribing them. Although abuse and dependence are not common with nonamphetamine appetite-suppressant medications, doctors should be cautious when they prescribe these medications for patients with a history of alcohol or other drug abuse.

Development of tolerance. Most studies of weight-loss drugs show that a patient's weight tends to level off after 6 months while still on medication. Although some patients and doctors may be concerned that this shows tolerance to the medications, the leveling off may mean that the medication is no longer effective. Based on the currently available studies, it is not clear if weight gain with continuing treatment is due to drug tolerance. A recent study found that orlistat aids in weight maintenance over a 3-year period, but more research is needed to confirm these findings and investigate other drugs.

Reluctance to make behavioral changes while using prescription medications. Patients who are overweight or obese should be able to seek medical treatment to prevent health risks that can cause serious illness and death. Weight-loss drugs, however, are not "magic bullets" or a one-shot fix for this chronic disease. They should always be combined with a healthy eating plan and increased physical activity.

Side Effects Exist

Because weight-loss drugs are used to treat a condition that affects millions of people, many of whom are basically healthy, the possibility that side effects may outweigh benefits is of great concern. Most side effects of these medications are mild and usually improve with continued treatment. Rarely, serious and even fatal outcomes have been reported. Some of the common side effects of medications are explained below.

Orlistat. Some side effects of orlistat include cramping, intestinal discomfort, passing gas, diarrhea, and leakage of oily stool. These side effects are generally mild and temporary, but may be worsened by eating high-fat foods. Also, because orlistat reduces the absorption of some vitamins, patients should take a multivitamin at least 2 hours before or after taking orlistat.

Sibutramine. The main side effects of sibutramine are increases in blood pressure and heart rate, which are usually small but may be of concern in some patients. Other side effects include headache, dry mouth, constipation, and insomnia. People with poorly controlled high blood pressure, heart disease, irregular heartbeat, or history of stroke should not take sibutramine, and all patients taking the drug should have their blood pressure monitored on a regular basis.

Other appetite suppressants. Phentermine, phendimetrazine, and diethylpropion may cause symptoms of sleeplessness, nervousness, and euphoria (feeling of well-being). People with heart disease, high blood pressure, an overactive thyroid gland, or glaucoma should not use these drugs.

Two appetite-suppressant medications, fenfluramine and dexfenfluramine, were withdrawn from the market in 1997. These drugs, used alone and in combination with phentermine (fen/phen) were linked to the development of valvular heart disease and primary pulmonary hypertension (PPH), a rare but potentially fatal disorder that affects the blood vessels in the lungs. There have been only a few case reports of PPH in patients taking phentermine alone, but the possibility that phentermine use is associated with PPH cannot be ruled out.

2

Obesity Drugs Might Be the Cure of the Future

New York Post

The New York Post *is the 13th-oldest U.S. newspaper and the 6th-largest U.S. newspaper by circulation.*

The side effects associated with current weight-loss medications are too severe to make them a viable medical solution for the general public, but a new crop of drugs might offer better treatment options for obese people. Obesity is putting a strain on the health care system. However, the potential use of weight-loss medications should not be viewed as a substitute for engaging in regular exercise and maintaining a healthy diet.

The race is on to find a magic fat pill.

Pharmaceutical companies are tripping over each other in their haste to develop new anti-obesity drugs. It's a ripe market: an estimated 97 million adults in the United States are obese.

Since 1991, adult obesity, defined as being about 30 pounds overweight, has risen an astounding 60 percent, according to the Centers for Disease Control.

Every year, about $30 billion is spent on weight-loss remedies in the United States alone. The U.S. market for prescription anti-obesity drugs rang up $296 million in 2000, according to health-care consulting firm IMS Health.

"It's an enticing market," acknowledged Louis Aronne, director of the Comprehensive Weight Control Center at New York Presbyterian Hospital.

"But the bottom line is, we need more medications out there. It's ridiculous to think you can make any inroads with obesity with the few drugs currently on the market."

Researchers at Houston's Baylor College of Medicine found that if an enzyme called ACC2 is blocked in mice, the animals can eat much more food than other mice and still weigh 10 to 15 percent less.

Here's a look at the most promising new research:

* *The Flu-Like Fat-Fighting Drug*
Ever notice that when you have the flu or a bad cold you're not hungry?
That's how researchers came up with the idea for Axokine, an appetite suppressant that mimics the effects of cytokines, hormones released by your body whenever you're ill or injured.
Clinical trials show that people on Axokine lost nearly 10 pounds over 12 weeks of treatment—and kept it off for at least six weeks after discontinuing the drug.
"At high doses, side effects include flu-like symptoms like nausea and coughing, but those reactions are rarely seen in patients treated with lower doses of Axokine," noted Steven Heymsfield, deputy director of the Obesity Research Center at St. Luke's Roosevelt Hospital.
Axokine, manufactured by Regeneron, could be available in two to three years.

* *Flipping the Appetite Switch "Off"*
While searching for a cure for cancer, researchers at Johns Hopkins Medical Institute may have unwittingly stumbled upon the solution to obesity.

The team discovered that when a synthetic compound called C75 was injected into mice, they lost much of their appetite and up to 30 percent of their body weight.

"C75 inhibits an enzyme called fatty acid synthase, which tricks the brain into thinking it's not hungry," Aronne said.

Another plus: the C75 mice lost more weight than fasting mice because their metabolism didn't slow down.

The researchers most likely will join forces with Baltimore technology company Fasgen Inc. to conduct human trials.

* *Pigging out without turning porky*

Eat all you want and lose weight!

Does that sound impossible? It worked with lab mice.

Researchers at Houston's Baylor College of Medicine found that if an enzyme called ACC2 is blocked in mice, the animals can eat much more food than other mice and still weigh 10 to 15 percent less.

"If it works in humans like it did in mice, I'd want it for myself," raved lead researcher Salih Wakil. "You could sit on the couch, eat to your heart's content, and still lose weight."

Wakil is now testing compounds that could be used in a pill to block ACC2. Human trials aren't expected for another five years.

* *Is Fat Contagious?*

Can a virus cause obesity?

Researchers have found that mice and chickens infected with adenovirus-36, a common human virus, put on much more fat than uninfected animals.

"Our studies also show that 20 to 30 percent of overweight humans are infected with adenovirus-36, compared to the general population," explained Nikhil Dhurander, a professor of medicine at Wayne State University in Detroit.

"We suspect it increases the number of fat cells, which encourages them to store more fat."

More study is needed. Eventually, obese people could be treated with anti-virals or possibly an anti-obesity vaccine.

* A Last Look at Leptin

Once seen as the key fighter in the anti-obesity battle, leptin was relegated to the sidelines once it proved to cause only moderate weight loss in humans.

But early studies suggest leptin, a form of human protein made in fat cells, is effective when combined with existing diet drugs such as Merida.

"You put people on Merida initially to lose weight, then switch them to leptin once they plateau," Heymsfield said.

3

Positive Lifestyle Choices Augment Weight-Loss Surgery

Patricia

Patricia is a health-care profesional who has undergone weight-loss surgery and has lost over 163 pounds.

Facing one's obesity and its associated health risks is a difficult prospect for people who have struggled with being overweight for most of their lives. Weight-loss surgery is an option for those who have already tried unsuccessfully to lose weight through diet and exercise. Before considering such a drastic procedure, however, one needs to research the pros and cons of weight-loss surgery and then consult a physician. It is important to understand that even after undergoing the surgery, one must be committed to altering one's lifestyle in order to sustain weight loss.

The realization that I am just one of millions of Americans challenged with being overweight does not intimidate me. In fact, it motivates me! You see, just one month ago, I shed the label of being "obese" by having exceeded a total weight loss of 163 lbs. following successful weight-loss surgery in January 2005. At 344 lbs. propelling me through life, I am now compelled by my life and enjoying every minute of this journey.

Obesity Hampered Fulfillment

Like so many of you, I have spent my lifetime struggling in a physical package that competed with my life goals and dreams. As an overweight child, I enjoyed playing sports, including

Patricia, "Turning the Mirror Inward ..." *Shape Up America!*, 2008. [www.shapeup.org] Reproduced by permission.

softball and volleyball, but had to work twice as hard to gain the physical endurance to play well and compete with the other kids. I was always picked last because what the other kids saw was the chubby girl not the hard-working, competitive athlete. The pain of being socially excluded always loomed and ultimately was insulated by the layers of fat that I began to accumulate. This vicious cycle propelled me into adulthood and presented even bigger challenges.

As I entered college, weighing in at 220 lbs, I was determined to become a registered nurse. I knew the childhood experience of having lost my father to heart disease when I was eight years old played into this decision along with a strong desire to help people since I seemingly couldn't help myself out of the depths of my own weight issues. As I reflect upon this now, I realize that I was merely deflecting my own failure in managing my weight into the positive of helping others with their own health challenges. The mirror is a powerful thing. I chose at that moment to turn it outward and stop looking inward.

I realized my weight was taking me down the road to being one of my own patients.

A New Self

My successful nursing career is colored with the many lives that I have been fortunate to touch and hopefully, make an impact on. As a critical care nurse, I was often faced with patients experiencing traumatic health issues and was extremely gratified to be able to help them in whatever way their circumstances dictated. I excelled in my bedside career and for the first time in my life, I wasn't first looked at as the "fat person" but rather as a "nurse." This new label felt good.

It wasn't long, though, before my desire to help others took me down a path of health and wellness. After having had such gratifying experiences working directly with patients, I soon realized that I needed to impact lives on a broader scale. I sought out professional opportunities that allowed me to create and deliver programs that would help people manage their chronic diseases such as asthma, diabetes, and heart disease, while living healthier. It was at this time that I realized my weight was taking me down the road to being one of my own patients.

Discussions about the efficacy and safety of weight-loss surgery always ended with my physician feeling that this was not a solution for me.

As I turned 39 years old, I was struck by how my weight was impacting normal, everyday activities. Having given up playing softball and volleyball years earlier because of the physical demands, things like riding my bike, walking through an airport and climbing a flight of stairs had now become a challenge. The realization that I was approaching the age at which my father's heart disease had taken his life, I knew that I had to take a more permanent step to control my weight beyond the numerous dieting attempts I had made over the years. The question became, was I ready to turn the mirror around and take a hard look at myself?

Helping Oneself

I can't point to one specific moment where I became ready to look at myself and actually do something significant about my obesity. For several years, I was aware of the advances being made in the area of weight-loss surgery but never considered this an option for me as it seemed so drastic. For two years, I spent numerous appointments with my primary care physician discussing my weight and trying different solutions. Discussions about the efficacy and safety of weight-loss surgery always ended with my physician feeling that this was not a solution for me. For some reason, though, the more I researched, the more I began to believe that this was exactly what I needed to pursue. In the fall of 2004, having garnered support from family and friends, I went into my physician's office armed with all of my research and validation for why this was the solution for me. Fortuitously, my physician had just completed a week-long training program in how to care for patients following weight-loss surgery. Her newly gained knowledge, coupled with my research, led us to agreement that I should proceed with having the procedure.

Vigilance Is Required

For those of you who have had the procedure or are actively pursuing it, you know how the next chapter of my story reads. Insurance qualification, a multitude of pre-surgical testing and preparation, post-surgical recovery and the astounding weight loss are now merely steps on the road to where I am today. There have been many lessons learned along this road but I want to share one of the most important ones here with you. Weight-loss surgery is less about anatomically changing one's digestive system and more about making life-long, sustainable, lifestyle changes. Please reread that last sentence. If you are not committed to making the lifestyle changes to support the new you, being successful long-term will forever be a challenge. Not a day goes by now where I don't pay attention to what I put in my mouth, and why, as well as making sure my activity level supports the needs of my new body. I am now compelled by my new label of "overweight" and rise to the challenge of looking in the mirror each and every day and realizing that I have the power to be successful.

As I look in the mirror, I finally see the physical me that reflects what's always been inside.

4

Obesity Surgery Can Have Serious Side Effects

Men's Health Advisor

Men's Health Advisor is a publication of the Cleveland Clinic, ranked in the top 10 of America's Best Hospitals by U.S. News & World Report.

It is important to understand all of the risks associated with weight-loss surgery prior to having the procedure done. Some of the risks include difficult-to-heal wounds, hernias, surgical complications, and corrective surgical procedures to address serious complications. Despite the potentially life-changing benefits of having weight-loss surgery, one should be cognizant of the fact that complications from surgery can be serious.

You've dieted. You've exercised. You've lost a little weight. You've put it back on. You're frustrated and depressed. More importantly, you're unhealthy.

This pattern is all too familiar for a burgeoning number of Americans. And, as the incidence of obesity has reached epidemic proportions, the popularity of bariatric surgery has grown just as dramatically. The surgery, which alters the gastrointestinal tract to limit the amount of food a person can eat, is the only method proven to help severely obese people achieve significant, long-term weight loss. Recognizing this fact, Medicare and many insurance companies now cover bariatric surgery.

Slightly more women than men are obese, but women undergo bariatric surgery 4 times as often as men. However, obesity is much more lethal in men than in women, a fact that experts like Philip Schauer, M.D., believe should prompt more obese men to consider surgery if other weight-loss options fail.

"It's funny, because we males, we go and get our prostate checked. We got that message. We get our stool checked for blood for colon cancer, and we get our heart checked, but we don't quite get the message that this obesity is killing us," said Dr. Schauer, director of The Cleveland Clinic Bariatric and Metabolic Institute.

BPD [biliopancreatic diversion] results in an average loss of 80 to 85 percent of excess weight in most patients. The surgery carries the greatest risk of long-term metabolic complications and nutritional deficiencies.

The Options

Bariatric operations are divided into 3 categories: restrictive, including laparoscopic adjustable gastric banding (LAGB), which reduces the capacity of the stomach; malabsorptive, including biliopancreatic diversion (BPD), which bypasses a large section of the intestinal tract; and a restrictive/malabsorptive combination known as Roux-en-Y gastric bypass (RYGB).

In LAGB, a surgeon places an inflatable inflatable silicone band around the upper stomach to form a small pouch. The band is attached to a port placed just below the skin and can be adjusted by injecting saline through the port. By tightening the band, the pouch empties more slowly, prolonging your feeling of fullness and curbing your appetite. LAGB, which comprises about 18 percent of the bariatric surgeries done in the U.S., is the simplest type to perform and carries the lowest risk of complications. Most patients lose an average of 45 to 50 percent of their excess weight. The LAGB procedure takes about an hour to complete, and most patients remain in the hospital 1 to 2 days.

BPD results in an average loss of 80 to 85 percent of excess weight in most patients. The surgery carries the greatest risk of long-term metabolic complications and nutritional deficiencies. Consequently, BPD generally is reserved for the most severely obese and comprises only about 2 percent of bariatric operations nationwide.

In RYGB, the most commonly performed bariatric surgery in the U.S., the surgeon staples the stomach near the esophagus, creating a small pouch, and bypasses the rest of the stomach and a small portion of the upper intestine. Most RYGB patients lose an average of 65 to 70 percent of their excess weight. The surgery takes about 2 hours to complete, and most patients can return home in 2 to 4 days.

The older you are and the higher your BMI [body-mass index] is, the greater your risk of surgical complications.

Some bariatric surgeons now use the laparoscopic approach, which allows for quicker recovery, less pain and fewer wound problems, such as infections or hernias. Laparoscopic surgery requires advanced training, however, so choose a surgeon experienced in this technique.

Is It for Me?

Studies show that bariatric surgery is the only method proven to help people lose large amounts of weight and keep it off after 10 years. The surgery also helps improve obesity-related conditions. As many as 83 percent of diabetes patients and 70 percent of people with high blood pressure achieve normal blood sugar and blood pressure levels without medication weeks to months after surgery. And, more than 80 percent of patients with high cholesterol will develop normal levels within 2 to 3 months. The surgery also has been shown to reduce pain in the back and leg joints and improve symptoms of asthma, sleep apnea, gallbladder disease and gastroesophageal reflux disease.

Before surgery, you'll undergo a medical examination, including a psychiatric and nutritional evaluation. In most bariatric programs, you'll attend seminars that inform you about the benefits and risks of the surgery and the lifestyle changes you'll need to make afterward.

You are a candidate for bariatric surgery if your body-mass index (BMI)—your weight in kilograms divided by your height in meters squared—is 40 or greater or if it is 35 or greater and you have a comorbidity such as high blood pressure, diabetes or sleep apnea. Also, you first must have tried to lose weight through diet, exercise or another conventional method.

The older you are and the higher your BMI is, the greater your risk of surgical complications. Severe medical conditions—such as severe heart disease, bleeding problems and psychological problems—may exclude you from bariatric surgery.

The most common complication associated with LAGB is a slipping of the band, which occurs in 5 to 10 percent of patients and requires a re-operation. Also, if the band is too tight and/or if patients eat too quickly, food may become obstructed in the pouch and trigger vomiting.

More serious complications after RYGB include bleeding (in less than 1 percent of patients) and intestinal leaks (2 to 3 percent). Due to rapid weight loss in the 6 months after RYGB, some patients develop gall stones and must take ursodiol (Actigall) to reduce or prevent their formation. Occasionally, some may require gallbladder removal.

Expect to see your doctor a week to 10 days after surgery and again a month later. Many patients must return to their doctor every 3 months within the first year of surgery and then once yearly afterward. Early on, LAGB patients may need to visit their doctor more frequently for band adjustments.

RYGB patients must take a multivitamin and iron, vitamin B-12 and calcium supplements after surgery, while LAGB patients need only a multivitamin. All bariatric surgery patients should not smoke and should avoid non-steroidal anti-inflammatory drugs such as ibuprofen (Motrin, Advil), naproxen (Aleve) and ketoprofen (Orudis), all of which may cause ulcers.

Most weight loss occurs 18 to 24 months after surgery. Some patients may regain some weight, usually 10 to 15 pounds over 10 years. Less than 5 percent of patients will regain most or all the weight.

Some patients go through such a change in their appearance that they suffer stress after surgery and may require counseling. Choose a bariatric program that has experienced surgeons and offers psychological support, as well as an educational component and dietary counseling.

Bariatric Surgery: Myths and Realities

Not everything you hear about bariatric surgery is accurate. Philip Schauer, M.D., director of The Cleveland Clinic Bariatric and Metabolic Institute, comments on the myths and realities of weight-loss surgery.

The Surgery Is Drastic and Risky.

A study of Medicare patients last fall concluded that the risk of early death after bariatric surgery is higher among men, older people, and patients of surgeons who have performed fewer bariatric procedures. The risk of death is still low, though, according to Dr. Schauer, and experienced surgeons can reduce the mortality rate to fewer than 4 in every 1,000 surgeries.

Bariatric Surgery Is Irreversible.

LAGB surgery is reversible through laparoscopic surgery to remove the band. RYGB is potentially reversible, but requires another surgery with the same risks. Bariatric operations are meant to be permanent and very few people seek reversals.

After Surgery, You No Longer Can Enjoy Good-Tasting Food.

"That's false. They'll just eat less food and still enjoy it," Dr. Schauer said. Still, patients must follow some specific eating guidelines. For example, RYGB patients should avoid high-calorie foods that may rapidly dump into the intestines and trigger cramps, diarrhea and nausea. Other foods—including steak, hamburgers, whole-grain or white bread, fruit skins and candy—may be difficult to tolerate after surgery.

If You Have Surgery, You'll Vomit and Suffer Diarrhea Frequently.

False. "Those side effects are uncommon," Dr. Schauer said.

Surgery Is The Solution, and It Requires No Self-Discipline Afterward.

Wrong. Bariatric surgery requires a commitment to changing your dietary and other lifestyle habits. Eating right and exercising are still keys to losing weight and keeping it off after surgery. "There are no perfect operations, and there are some people who don't apply any discipline and can have a less-than-desirable result," Dr. Schauer said.

5

Staying Active Is Key to Losing Weight

Obesity Focused

Obesity Focused is an Internet-based resource aimed at providing up-to-date and accurate information about healthy lifestyle choices for obese people.

For most people, engaging in an active lifestyle is the best way to lose excess weight. Many people believe that joining a health club and working out with a personal trainer is an ideal way to exercise, but for those who might be too obese to participate in a strenuous workout, taking walks is a viable alternative to going to the gym. The important thing is to turn your back on a sedentary lifestyle and get moving.

Staying active has become a national battle cry and it's largely because obesity has become a huge public health concern. Data shows that up to fifty percent of people in most states are obese. While poor diet cannot be ignored, inactivity is a large component of the problem. Physical education programs get cut in schools to save money, families lead busy lifestyles and computer work and television occupy our time. Staying active is not as easy as it sounds.

Trainers, Gyms, and Working Out

When most people think of staying active or exercising they picture a grueling workout at the gym every day. The assumption is that intense exercise will lead to fast weight loss as

Obesity Focused, "Lose Weight Through Exercise and Staying Active," Obesity Focused, August, 2008. Reproduced by permission.

calories are burned like crazy. While using a gym is a fantastic way to lose weight, so many people enter a gym with unrealistic expectations. Trying to do too much too soon leaves us exhausted, achy and lacking in motivation. The fast weight loss we dreamed of doesn't materialize, and we stop going to the gym. In doing so, we forfeit any exercise-related weight loss and other health benefits.

In fact, a good trainer will advise you not to start working out at such a break-neck (or sprained muscle) pace. Instead, he or she will suggest you start light cardiovascular training three days a week to slowly build up strength while staying active on a daily basis. Not only is this more manageable, you're less likely to have training injuries and more likely to keep it up.

If you need motivation, consider walking with a friend or family member.

One other note if you go to the gym to lose weight: Throw out your scale. Staying active burns fat, sure, but also builds muscle. Muscle weighs far more than fat, so though you might be healthier and in better shape, you might actually gain weight over the first few months! Ditch the scales in favor of a measuring tape if you want to chart your progress.

Staying Active Means Getting Up

Lets face the facts: While the gym works wonders for most people, if you are very overweight or obese, even light gym training may prove too strenuous for you. Not to mention how self-conscious you feel training next to Buffy the Tai Bo Queen.

The truth is, staying active doesn't require a gym membership, or even intense exercise. In fact, for many of us who lead sedentary lives, staying active just means getting up and moving around!

Experts recommend thirty minutes of exercise daily. This doesn't mean it all needs to be done in one fell swoop. Staying active for 10 minutes at a time three to four times a day and building up the amount of time slowly is a great way to introduce your body to exercise.

Walking to lose weight works, but it takes a long time before you see any visible results.

Walking for Exercise and Weight Loss

When asked, doctors often suggest walking as the best exercise for obese patients.

If you need motivation, consider walking with a friend or family member. An evening walk can become a wonderful way to catch up on the events of the day, and the company makes it more enjoyable. If you can't find someone to walk with, bring along some music as a diversion.

Most people start walking, but quickly give up on the idea. Why? Walking to lose weight works, but it takes a long time before you see any visible results. So it's hard to get out there every day—feels like you're doing all the work for nothing. Consider changing your thinking. Rather than focusing on weight loss, think of exercise as a step to becoming healthy. Results may not be instant but they are enduring and contribute to slow and steady weight loss.

Here are a few other ideas for staying active:

- Mow the lawn.

- Play a few holes of golf.

- Shoot some hoops.

- Take a water exercise class.

- Chose a distant parking spot.

Measuring Steps

For some, staying active means employing pedometers to measure steps. Available at various prices and accuracies, pedometers can be clipped to clothing and act as step counters. At its best, pedometers give the wearer a better picture of daily activity. According to health experts, for every 2,000 steps 100 calories are burned. A recommended 10,000 steps per day for good fitness translates into approximately five miles and the prevention of a ten-pound weight gain every year.

People who use pedometers report that staying active is easy when they have a goal to work towards. If the number falls short of the 10,000 steps at the end of the day, they add an extra walk to meet their goal.

6

A Food Diary Can Help with Weight Loss

Lee Kern

Lee Kern is the clinical director for Structure House, a residential weight loss facility in Durham, North Carolina.

To maintain the weight-loss resulting from surgery, patients have to stay vigilant for the rest of their lives. One important tool is a food diary. If properly kept, the food diary can become a valuable partner in helping patients to overcome poor eating habits. In addition, the food diary does not have to be just a tool to monitor meals or count calories; it also can be used to track changes in body weight and to log an exercise program.

What do Simon and Garfunkel, Lennon and McCartney, Abbott and Costello, and Burns and Allen have in common? These icons of music and comedy rose to greatness through partnerships in which the collective creative sum was greater than their parts. Successful lifelong weight control works much the same way. To ensure long-term success you must partner your surgery with other tools. One of the most powerful tools is the food diary, frequently recommended by nutritionists and behavior therapists, yet at the same time the bane of most dieters' existence. Diaries are avoided because they require time, attention, planning, and analysis, yet their ability to enhance success is supported by numerous studies. Perhaps the best resolution to this paradox is to view the diary as your faithful partner and accept that this alliance will produce what you cannot do alone.

Lee Kern, "The Food Diary: A Partner To Success," *Obesity Treatment*, 2008. Reproduced by permission of the author.

Keeping Track of Meals

Consider the results from a study whose overweight subjects saw themselves as doing everything right toward losing weight, yet they were not losing. Subjects were asked to use "recall"—to remember everything they had been eating. The findings indicated that the average person recalls only half of what they eat, meaning that without the aid of an external tracking device, we do not attend to our entire food intake. We consume many calories unconsciously—we nibble at the fridge or the sink, we snack while on the phone or in the car, we graze while watching television. Call it denial or inattentiveness—all these calories add up and can undermine our efforts to lose the next pound. A food diary puts a stop to this lack of accountability and becomes a partner to the commitment to heighten awareness of what we do with food. If success is like building a house, then this level of honesty is its solid foundation.

I consider a food diary to be a bit like a Swiss Army Knife—one tool that can perform many useful functions. While a diary can be done in a variety of ways, there are several targets that will be hit if it is done properly. Those targets include the following: meal planning, food tracking, calorie consciousness, identifying unwanted eating, trigger awareness, weight monitoring, exercise and benefits log. Let's look at these in more detail.

Meal Planning

Many weight loss and obesity experts have concluded that this culture has become a "toxic food environment." It is a food jungle out there and the best way to get through it safely is to have a written plan for meals for each day before the day starts. Overeaters simply cannot afford to leave things up to the last minute and say, "what do I feel like having?" A meal plan is like a map that makes it more likely you will get to your destination.

Food Tracking

Let's face it—not all eating will go according to plan. The diary needs to be a way of tracking everything that is consumed, whether on or off the plan. If you eat what is on the plan, then be sure to record the quantities or portion sizes. For off-plan eating, you need to write things down as soon afterward as possible: including what, and how much was eaten. In the end, the diary is a record of everything you eat, planned and unplanned.

A food diary enables the user to take an in-depth look at the relationship with food, and heightening awareness of the reasons for unwanted eating.

Calorie Consciousness

While magic diets come and go, most nutritionists recognize the basic energy equation of "calories in/calories out" as fundamental to weight loss over the long run. Therefore, part of effective diary keeping is accounting for the calories in the food consumed. Calorie awareness needs to be part of the meal plan as well. Meals should be balanced, maximizing nutrition, and designed to hit a daily calorie target that will result in either maintaining the weight lost, or a slow and steady rate of losing weight.

Identifying Unwanted Eating

Driver's education teaches us that when we approach an intersection that has a yellow blinking light, we should slow down and pay careful attention. Proper use of a diary should distinguish between on-target (within the plan) and off-target (outside of the plan) eating. If we assume that the planned eating was balanced, nutritious and designed to meet daily nourishment, then unplanned eating is likely to be using food to meet non-nourishment needs. The diary is a beacon that highlights food misuse and serves as a signal to slow down and pay attention.

Exercise improves health and fitness, burns calories, boosts the metabolism, and maybe most importantly helps create the right mindset.

Trigger Awareness

A food diary enables the user to take an in-depth look at the relationship with food, and heightening awareness of the reasons for unwanted eating. Was it repetitive habit eating that occurs at the same time every day? Was it an automatic response to food cues? Was it using food to entertain or reward? Was it eating to escape, distract or numb emotions or stress? These questions enable a food diary to stretch beyond planning and tracking, becoming a tool for self-reflection. Insights gained from this process become the foundation for relapse prevention.

Weight Monitoring

Experts have differing opinions about the role of the scale in weight loss. Some believe in frequent weighing, some do not. One way to resolve this question is to study "successful losers" to see what they do. Perhaps the largest study of successful people is the National Weight Control Registry, which is tracking more than 4,000 weight losers for more than 12 years. One common denominator that links many of these subjects is frequent (often daily) weighing. Don't ignore what works for so many; your diary keeping should include a way for you to record (and graph if you like) your daily or frequent weights.

Exercise and Benefits Log

Another finding from the National Registry is that successful losers are active exercisers. Exercise improves health and fitness, burns calories, boosts the metabolism, and maybe most importantly helps create the right mindset. I have heard clients say they refrained from a binge by remembering the calories burned in that morning's exercise session. Using the diary to record all your exercise will help you see the big picture of change and progress. There are other long-term markers of success to track, too. For example, one of my clients noted when she could first go up a flight of stairs, instead of using the elevator, and another client cited her first plane flight without needing the seat belt extension. This use of the diary ensures that you will see the forest of accumulated benefits and not just the tree of today's weight.

When it comes to long-term weight control, no man or woman is an island. Strength of character and willpower are useful qualities to draw on, but they are not enough. You need to partner your surgery with tools, strategies and support systems that will empower your efforts. Making a food diary your partner will improve your ability to plan and monitor your food intake, as well as heighten your awareness and help you appreciate the benefits of your hard work.

7

A Culture Obsessed with Thinness Propagates Misconceptions About Obesity

Amy Moon

Amy Moon is a features editor for the San Francisco Chronicle.

Our culture is obsessed with thinness, and millions of Americans attempt to achieve this ideal through diets and weight-loss treatments. At the same time, obesity is reaching epidemic proportions in the United States, even affecting children. The irony is that while the mainstream media glamorizes thinness and the pursuit of a healthy lifestyle as indicators of physical beauty and success in life, the food industry also uses the media to bombard consumers with advertisements for high-fat, convenient foods that inevitably contribute to unhealthy weight gain. In turn, the weight-loss industry promotes the ideal of thinness in order to sell their diet products and medical procedures to consumers who are unhappy with their own physical appearance and feel compelled to lose weight. However, recent studies have shown that poor diet and lack of exercise are just two of many factors that contribute to obesity, including genetic make-up, psychological disorders, and class status. In fact, researchers now believe that physical appearance is not always the best indicator of fitness and that often overweight, yet active people enjoy a relatively healthy lifestyle. For many, the larger issue is changing deeply ingrained cultural attitudes that unfairly stigmatize obese people.

Amy Moon, "Our Big Fat Fear: America's Obesity Epidemic Goes Hand in Hand with Fat Phobia," *SF Gate*, April 8, 2008. Reproduced by permission.

I once worked with a woman who told her husband when they got married that if she got fat, he could "take her out back and shoot her."

She's not alone in her fear of fat. Even though the major news being trumpeted everywhere these days is about the U.S. obesity epidemic, there is an equal if not greater epidemic of fat phobia in this country. In fact, *fear* isn't a strong enough word: We hate fat.

A Cultural Obsession

For evidence, one needs only to look at any number of magazines and television ads featuring models flaunting their flabless abs, pecs and tushes or touting the latest weight-loss miracle, or to peruse the most recent issue of *Star* magazine, whose cover story asks, "Kirstie Alley—What happened and why!?!" Apparently, the formerly sexy star of "Cheers" has ballooned up to 275 pounds. The magazine includes grainy photos of Alley's favorite fast-food stops, including the House of Pies and an In-N-Out burger place. There was even a humiliating shot of her stuffing herself with tacos in her car. She's not having a torrid affair with the swimming-pool maintenance man; worse yet, she's eating herself to death in floral tent dresses!

At the same time, we read distressing stories about the skyrocketing rates of diabetes, heart disease and high blood pressure, all tied to obesity. The U.S. surgeon general has stated that obesity may soon overtake tobacco as the leading cause of preventable deaths in this country, and an oft-cited figure from the U.S. Centers for Disease Control and Prevention is that more than 60 percent of adults in the United States are now overweight, and one third of those are obese.

(Since 1998, the official U.S. National Institutes of Health measure of weight status in adults is based on body-mass index, or BMI, calculated by dividing weight in kilograms by height in meters squared. A BMI below 18.5 is considered underweight, a measure of 18.5–24.9 is normal, a 25.0–29.9 tally is overweight and a figure of 30.0 and above is obese.)

Children Are Affected

The number of fat children with corresponding health problems is also on the rise: About 15 percent of children and adolescents are now overweight, a percentage that has more than doubled since the early 1970s. Even our pets are overweight. A recent *USA Today* magazine includes the headline, "How to help your fat dog," and a co-worker of mine was ordered by her cat's veterinarian to put it on a Catkins diet.

Although there's no doubt Americans have gotten bigger and fatter, outweighing people in most other countries and incurring potential health risks, how much cause for concern do we really have? In this cultural frenzy over obesity, is there some measure of capitalist-fueled fat-phobic claptrap that sells magazines and newspapers and fuels our mega food and diet industry because it feeds into our fears about being fat? I mean, is being fat really so bad?

A Chronicle *story about doughnuts gets the third-highest number of page views of any story on* SF Gate *that day, a ranking usually reserved for sports, sex or scandal.*

Too Many Food Choices

It's fairly standard knowledge that the reason we are getting fatter is because we're eating super-size portions of bad food and not exercising enough. Who can blame us? The American landscape is full of tantalizing food at every turn. Fast food, snack food, concessions to accompany every activity, vending machines everywhere, 7-Elevens, 24-hour gas and food marts, take-out, drive-thru. Food made easy. Candy bars turned into bags of little nuggets that you can easily tip into your mouth, chips that come in big 3.5-serving individual-size bags, food you can eat in your car or at your desk, no utensils necessary. And let's not forget about food porn: There's the Food Channel, with shows about food all day and all night, and the new cult of celebrity chefs such as Jamie Oliver, Nigella Lawson and Mario Batalli, who garner as much worship as movie stars.

Several books put the blame for our weight problem squarely on the food industry and warn readers to take heed. In *Food Fight: The Inside Story of the Food Industry, America's Obesity Crisis and What We Can Do About It*, authors Kelly D. Brownell and Katherine Battle Horgen, experts on nutrition, obesity and eating disorders, proclaim that Americans are succumbing to the ready availability of "toxic" food, which will lead inevitably to obesity, disability and early death. Meanwhile, Marion Nestle, author of *Food Politics: How the Food Industry Influences Nutrition and Health*, culls from her experience on a number of federal committees dealing with food, nutrition and policy matters to relate how government dietary standards are not created out of concern for our health. They are susceptible to a whole host of influences mostly from big business.

Food Industry Profits from Obesity

A review by Amazon.com states, "Central to her argument is the American 'paradox of plenty,' the recognition that our food abundance leads profit-fixated food producers to do everything possible to broaden their market portion, thus swaying us to eat *more* when we should do the opposite."

Honestly, though, don't we all know this already? And yet the food is right there, tempting us at every turn. I find myself taking a break at work and reading a story in the *New York Times* about the best cheesecake in the city. I even find myself clicking to view the multimedia cheesecake show. A *Chronicle* story about doughnuts gets the third-highest number of page views of any story on *SF Gate* that day, a ranking usually reserved for sports, sex or scandal. And NPR [National Public Radio] reports that Red Lobster had to stop offering its all-you-can-eat buffet. Apparently, it's become a money loser, because people are eating so much. A friend of mine remarked, "It's like we have no shame anymore." Food is a national pastime. No wonder we're getting bigger.

Fat Is Complicated

In *Fat Land: How Americans Became the Fattest People in the World*, author Greg Critser cites James O'Hill, physiologist at the University of Colorado's Health Sciences Center, who says being obese is a normal response to the current American environment. He adds that the percentage of overweight people has always been a relatively stable 25 percent of the population. But, he says, beginning in the late '80s, we started seeing that rate spike upward to 30, 35 and 40 percent.

Delving beneath these figures and the obvious junk-food/sedentary-lifestyle factors, one is still faced with the question of who is fat and why. That's where it gets complicated. It seems there are as many reasons for why a person is fat as there are fat people.

There is very little access to healthful food in lower-income areas.

Some people are just genetically predisposed to being heavier. A nutrition-savvy friend of mine put it this way: Let's say a person metabolizes 100 calories a day less than his friend Joe. Given that you gain a pound of fat for every extra 3,500 calories you take in, that person eating the same amount as Joe would gain a pound every 35 days (100 calories x 35 days = 3,500 calories) which equates to about 7 pounds over the course of a year, and many more over the course of a lifetime. Obviously, it wouldn't work exactly like that, but, nonetheless, this example goes to show that, over time, seemingly minor differences in metabolic effectiveness could lead to pretty substantial differences in weight.

Mental Disorders Might Contribute to Obesity

But fat goes deeper than that. Although some obese people may be genetically predisposed to being overweight, other heavier people are simply eating more. And, whereas many in our thin-obsessed, judgment-prone society may feel that's because fat people just don't care or have no self-control, that is often not the case. According to the Web site of Dr. Michael D. Myers, who has lectured about and treated obesity and eating disorders since 1980, more than 30 percent of individuals seeking medical treatment for obesity and (in some surveys) up to half of individuals being seen in nonmedical weight-reduction programs meet the criteria for binge eating disorder, which is also frequently (50 percent of the time) associated with major depression.

Mirasol, a center for recovery from eating disorders and chronic illness, describes the causes of binge eating on its Web site: "In general, binge eating results when a person is experiencing emotional pain at a level of intensity that she does not know how to manage in a healthy way, mainly because she did not learn to express feelings directly while growing up." In addition, the site states that eating disorders tend to be complex and may be caused by family and cultural pressures as well as psychological and interpersonal factors. Feelings of inadequacy, depression, anxiety and loneliness and difficult family and personal relationships may all play a part. . . .

Fat Might Be a Class Issue

The issue of fat is further complicated by socioeconomic factors: Obesity and overweight disproportionately plague the poor and working poor. The reasons are complicated as well.

First of all, there is very little access to healthful food in lower-income areas. (During graduate school, when I lived in South Central Los Angeles, I was naively shocked by the limited food options in my neighborhood stores—it was mostly off-brand junk food, white bread and canned foods—and how expensive it was. In my ignorance, I think I assumed prices would be lower because the food was of poorer quality.) Studies have shown that when low-income people have access to higher-quality food, their health levels improve.

Also, according to Greg Critser, people with less education and lower income levels receive lower-quality medical care, health practitioners are not as likely to inform them about the dangers of obesity and they are less likely to receive diagnostic tests in a timely manner. They may also be less likely to visit a doctor in the first place. The authors of *Food Fight* also note that for many lower-income people, discrimination causes anxiety, which makes people turn to food for comfort, which in turn makes them fat and less likely to be steadily employed, prompting a cycle of less security and further fueling discrimination and anxiety.

Thin Is In

At the same time that the poor and undereducated are getting fatter, thinness has become increasingly equated with wealth and success. After all, how many fat top executives can you think of? How many fat wealthy socialites and playboys? Movie stars? Celebrities of all types are generally thin. And, because of this fact, we tend to think of thinness itself as a sign of success.

In *Fat Land*, Critser quotes Jane Gallop, distinguished professor of English at the University of Wisconsin at Milwaukee, who commented in the *New York Times*, "If the right wing is moralistic about sex, the left is moralistic about food—that's where the new style of moralism about control is. Well-educated people are supposed to be in control of the amount of body fat they have. The people who are disgusted by [former president Bill] Clinton and Monica's [Lewinsky] fat aren't the right wing; they're the ones who wanted a yuppie president with the right amount of body fat at the helm." I don't agree with Gallop's assessment that it's the left wing, however; I think it's successful people of any political stripe and, more specifically, people who want to be perceived as successful (and who among us doesn't?), that hate fat and fat people.

Being thin is a visual cue to others that we are able and willing to get what we want. This goes for men as well as women these days, although the pressure is still predominantly on females.

In any number of surveys that appear in women's magazines, the obsession to be thin is evident. Rader Programs, a center for treatment of eating disorders, lists several examples. Among them, one survey showed that three out of four women stated that they were overweight, although only one out of four actually were. Another found that adolescent girls were more fearful of gaining weight than getting cancer, experiencing nuclear war or losing their parents.

Fat people have become the human embodiment of the dark side of our thin-obsessed perfectionism, a reminder of our own vulnerabilities.

Fear Plays into the Hands of the Diet Industry

This obsession fuels the $40 billion-a-year diet industry. And, according to a story on personal-finance Web site Bankrate-.com, there are no signs of a slowdown. Although nearly 55 million Americans will go on some kind of diet this year, only 5 to 10 percent will succeed, which means that next year, 90 to 95 percent may want to try again. By 2006, diet-industry revenues are expected to top $48 billion.

The low success rates from weight-loss programs show something most of us have heard before and yet continue to ignore: Diets don't work. In fact, many claim diets are responsible for making people fatter than they would be if they had never dieted in the first place.

Despite all the studies about our increasing girth and the calls to action, the reasons for obesity and overweight remain mysterious. "No one chooses to be obese, and the evidence is accumulating that it is a process that, once started, takes on a life of its own," says Louis Aronne, director of the weight-control program at Weill-Cornell Medical Center in Manhattan and president-elect of the North American Association for the Study of Obesity in an article about that subject for *Vogue* magazine.

Fat people have become the human embodiment of the dark side of our thin-obsessed perfectionism, a reminder of our own vulnerabilities. As a friend said, "When I see a fat person, I think, 'There but for the grace of God go I.'" We hate fat people not because of who they are but because of what we fear we might be. Fat people are pariahs whose shame is visible for all to see. They are the receptacle for all of our fears of not being good enough.

The Fat-Positive Movement

At 5'4″ and 275 pounds, Marilyn Wann is one of the leading lights of the fat-positive movement. Wann is the creator of *Fat!So?*, originally a zine, now a Web site and book that caters to the empowerment of fat people. In a society rife with mistrust and scorn for the fat, Wann is a revolutionary in a new civil rights movement.

Her own experience with fat discrimination led her to the freedom-fighting path she's on. "I started Fat!So? because of what I call my really bad day," says Wann. "Two things happened [that day.] I was having dinner with this guy, and, in the middle of dinner, he said, 'Wow, I just realized I'm embarrassed to introduce you to some of my friends because you're fat.'" That night, she suggested he read some books about fat empowerment. "But, of course, he couldn't change his attitude, and we didn't date any longer," she says.

"Fitness, not fatness, is the more important issue."

The second incident immediately followed the first one, Wann says. "That night, [after the date,] I came home and opened my mail and just thought, 'Well, I'll open the mail and go to bed, and tomorrow I'll be past this painful stuff,' right? But in the mail, Blue Cross of California sent me a letter saying, 'Thanks so much for your interest in Blue Cross, but you're morbidly obese, and we're unwilling to give you health insurance at any price.'"

In the Closet

Wann pauses and takes a deep breath, before adding, "I'm a pretty smart, fun person, and I had developed what I think of as survival skills around being a fat person, which mainly involved never talking about it. I liken it to being in the closet—even though it's no secret, right? But I would never talk about it; I would never say the F-word, *fat*. I never went on diets, because I just found it too humiliating to say, 'Oh, I'm so fat, I need to lose weight,' right? And so I was good at school, and I was really funny and smart and had a bunch of friends, but there was kind of this black hole in the area about my weight that I just never went into, because there just didn't seem to be anything good to come out of going there, right? So, because of that really bad day, I decided—as Audre Lourde so brilliantly says, 'Our silence doesn't protect us'—I decided to speak out."

Since the publication of the first issue of *Fat!So?*, Wann has received many heartbreaking letters from people telling her that reading her words made them feel OK for the first time in their lives. She has also often been in the media spotlight because, as she says, "the media is so fascinated in a prurient way with a fat person who says she's happy."

Fat and Fit

Fat empowerment is all well and good, but what about all the disease and health problems fat people are faced with? Wann firmly believes lifestyle factors, rather than weight, determine a person's level of health, and that health practitioners who focus on weight as an indicator of health status are doing a huge disservice not only to the health of fat people but also to that of thin people. She says, "I'm healthy because I feel good, because I like my body and my personal metabolic numbers all happen to be normal—meaning blood pressure, blood sugars and cholesterol."

Wann's beliefs are supported by research conducted by Steven Blair, Ed.D., of the Cooper Institute for Aerobics Research in Dallas and senior scientific editor of the "U.S. Surgeon General's Report on Physical Activity and Health" in 1996. In a story for *Runner's World*, Blair says, "Fitness, not fatness, is the more important issue." In the article, Blair states that he bases his conclusions on years of research conducted at the Cooper Institute, studying the relationship of cardiorespiratory fitness to mortality in men grouped by BMI. His studies show that death rates were significantly higher in men with low fitness levels, regardless of BMI, whereas death rates of men at all BMI levels who were moderately or very fit were similar. In fact, Blair says he found that men with low fitness levels who had a BMI of less than 27 were at greater risk for death than very fit men with a BMI over 30.

Professor Glenn Gaesser, director of kinesiology at the University of Virginia and author of the book *Big Fat Lies:*

The Truth about Your Weight and Your Health, echoes Blair's findings. In an e-mail exchange with me, Gaesser states, "Many obese persons (using the standard of BMI over 30) are healthier than their thinner counterparts. It is quite possible—and has been documented in the literature—that obese men and women can outperform many thin people in measures of endurance and strength, and also have better lipid profiles, glucose tolerance, insulin sensitivity and blood pressures, etc."

Extremely healthy people are not immune from early death.

Obesity Might Be Misrepresented

According to Gaesser, "When you get out to the extremes of obesity, e.g., BMI over 40, it becomes harder to find truly "fit and fat" persons. But those with BMIs over 40 constitute less than 5 percent of the total overweight/obese population. When you get down to the men and women closer to a BMI of 30, it becomes much harder to say that obesity categorically is harmful."

Gaesser concludes by saying, "Fitness and health may not come in *all* sizes and shapes, but it certainly is possible to come in *many* sizes and shapes. Furthermore, the risks associated with dieting, almost invariably of the yo-yoing type, and other sometimes drastic weight-loss measures, may be greater than the risks of obesity itself."

Although morbid obesity seems unhealthy, if only for the reality of physically having to sustain and tote an extra 100-plus pounds—the pressure on organs and joints seems immense—medical evidence appears to support the idea that for those on the heavy side, it is not our weight that is the main indicator of health, but, rather, our lifestyle. Gaesser and others have done research showing that when overweight people improve their diet and exercise, overall health can drastically improve without any corresponding weight loss.

Empirical evidence also seems to support the idea that people can be healthy at very different weights. Look around. Some fat people look healthy; others look unhealthy. Some thin people look healthy; others look unhealthy. While this layperson's approach to health evaluation may seem specious at best, let's face it: Health is a complicated matter. Extremely healthy people are not immune from early death. Marathon runner Jim Fixx, one of the champions of the fitness-running craze in the '70s, died at 52 of a heart attack while running, as did Brian Maxwell, a fitness enthusiast and the creator of the Power Bar, who recently collapsed in a San Anselmo, California, post office at age 51.

That the idea of a fat fit person has not caught on like gangbusters is a sign of our wishful thinking. On some level, we want to believe it's dangerous to be fat. That assumption gives us fuel for our desire to be thin and a concrete and scientific reason for our scorn for fat people. We cling to our biases even though it hurts us, too.

Ultimately, fat phobia affects not just fat people, but all of us. Natalie Boero, a Ph.D. candidate in sociology at UC Berkeley, is writing her dissertation on the "social construction of the obesity epidemic." Boero, a member of the Padded Lilies, a group of fat synchronized-swimming enthusiasts, says she doesn't identify as obese, even though her BMI puts her in that range.

"I'm teaching a course at UC Berkeley called The Sociology of Body Size, and my students, many of whom fit the ideal, absolutely feel like s— about their bodies," says Boero. "We talk about fat discrimination, and, yes, the tangible effects of this discrimination are felt more by fat people. However, the internal self-hatred is often the same for thin people, because, fat or thin, we grow up in this same culture."

And Boero sees the fat-phobic culture spreading. "I think as Western influence spreads around the world, both pieces of it spread—fast-food culture and fat-phobic culture," she says. Within America, Boero adds, certain groups are more tolerant of fatness, but, she says, that's changing, too. "I'm a lesbian, and I think, in terms of body acceptance, there are more sort of acceptable varieties, but I fear that it's changing," she says. "It's similar to African-American society: Now you read *Essence* magazine, and there are more diet stories, and the models get thinner and thinner. Men, too. It's not as all encompassing for men, but that's changing. I think the Atkins diet is bringing men in."

Retailers are realizing there's a big market out there of big people who want to dress well.

She sees the impact on her students as well: "My students, they are racially and ethnically diverse, diverse class backgrounds, ages, sizes—and they all feel it. This is not a class full of 18-year-old, upper-middle-class white girls who feel the pressure. It's not. It's everywhere."

Freedom Fighter

Marilyn Wann's fight for freedom from fat oppression may seem to be for her own benefit or to voice a grievance from a small group. But her work is larger than that. She likens fat phobia to other kinds of oppression such as racism, sexism, homophobia, ageism and religious intolerance. "They are all felt differently, but the process is kind of the same, and I want all of us to be free of all of that," she says. "And, as long as any one of these awful divisions of humans against humans continues, they all still get a little juice. Especially, on the weight thing, I really think the traditional us-versus-them—thin people versus fat people—just isn't where it's at. That's not the conflict, because I don't know very many thin people who feel OK in their bodies."

"I don't envy thin people; I don't fear thin people; I'm not angry at thin people," Wann adds. "I'm angry at our society for continuing to promote this way of thinking, and I think that all of us in our individual bodies, in our individual lives, can divest from that hateful way of thinking, just like people divested from apartheid."

"It's a long process," she says. "I think people feel hopeless in the face of a societal attitude. They feel like, 'Who am I? I can't do anything to change this big thing. Instead, I'll try to change my thighs.' And, actually, it's much easier and more possible and more effective and more fun to change the world than it is ever to change your body to fit a hateful standard."

The Cure Is in the Disease

Maybe the very thing that gets us obsessed about food and fat—our own consumer culture—will help us to stop. For all the diets being espoused these days, there are also signs of acceptance. Retailers are realizing there's a big market out there of big people who want to dress well. Perhaps this trend means that some of us are getting off the self-hating yo-yo diet treadmill and realizing we're never going to be thin. And, once you accept your size, you can start living and start looking good.

Plus-size-clothing catalogues are more common. Harper Greer, which caters to women sizes 12 and above, just opened on Berkeley's fashionable Fourth Street. And *Vogue* magazine's latest issue [April, 2004] is all about fashion at any size. There are tips for how to dress if you are pear shaped, have no waist or petite or thin, and now there is a new category: curvy! Elsewhere in the magazine, sexy, sultry Carre Otis, formerly thin model and Mickey Rourke's ex, is modeling plus-size clothing in glamorous ads for high-end designer Marina Rinaldi, whose slogan is "Style is not a size . . . it's an attitude." (Ironically, Rinaldi's sizes start at size 10, smaller than the average woman, and Otis looks kind of thin to me.)

Perhaps a small shift is occurring in the cultural land-scape. I remember, back in 1992, looking at *Vanity Fair*'s Steven Meisel photo spread of Madonna in innocent, childlike erotic poses and wondering, What more could she possibly do?

I remember thinking that the most radical thing Madonna could do next would be to get fat. Of course, she instead became a devout Kabbalah devotee and a wife, mother and children's-book author. But I still think getting fat would have been it. That sentiment may seem super shallow, but sometimes the deepest, most lasting things start out that way.

8

A Tax on High Fat Foods Might Modify Poor Eating Habits

Anatoly Karlin

Anatoly Karlin is the author of a blog that concentrates on Russian news topics, as well as on subjects of general interest.

The government should implement a graduated tax system on foods high in fat to counteract the obesity epidemic. Such a program would persuade people to cut back drastically on fat- and sodium-rich foods and encourage them to start eating food that is good for them. The goal is not to increase the life expectancy of the population but to make people live healthier and more productive lives.

We noticed that culinary cultures which consume a low-fat diet tend to have dramatically lower mortality rates from CVDs [cardiovascular diseases] and degenerative diseases than those who indulge in a high-fat, high-sodium 'civilized' diet. As such it is a good idea to encourage consumption to shift from high-fat to low-fat foods.

Taxing Fatty Foods

Research should be conducted so as to ascertain the optimal levels of taxation to maximize positive outcomes, and the tax will probably be introduced gradually. But I'll give a rough idea of how the tax will work below.

Anatoly Karlin, "We Need a Fat Tax," Da Russophile, April 19, 2008. Reproduced by permission.

Calculate the caloric fat content of a particular food (take the number of grams of fat per 100g and multiply by 9; divide this by calories per 100g to get %). Anything under 20% will remain untaxed. This includes vegetables, fruits, fish and some white meats (skinless chicken breast). Then a flat tax of 25% for 20–30% fat (this will account for leaner steaks), 100% for 30–50% fat (traditional red meats) and 200% for 50+% fat (fast food hamburgers, vegetable oils, etc).

It goes without saying that advertising unhealthy foods will be a no-no, along with alcoholic drinks and tobacco.

Sodium will be taxed too. The RDA [recommended daily allowance] for sodium is 2g, or 4g of salt (max 3g/6g). Say, anything with more than 0.5g of sodium [per] 100g will be flat taxed at 50%.

A few foods, while OK in fat, are unacceptably high in cholesterol. The big one [is] eggs—one egg yolk = 2 days of RDA of cholesterol. Tax them at 200%. While some seafoods like prawns or oysters are medium-high in cholesterol, they have other health benefits, so leave them untaxed. I will not tax sugar because a) cakes, puddings, etc will already be taxed for their fat content and b) a lot of fruit actually contains a rather high % of sugar, but it is of a healthy kind. Fruit shouldn't be taxed.

Advertising Restrictions

It is of course vital to propagandize the benefits for personal health of a low-fat diet on prime-time TV, radio, Internet and other media outlets. It goes without saying that advertising unhealthy foods will be a no-no, along with alcoholic drinks and tobacco. On the other hand, people do respond to price signals, and meat and sweets costing less than fruit does not make a good contribution to public health. The fact is that countries with some specific diets (e.g. Okinawans have a life expectancy of 85 years) have health results that are objectively better than countries with other diets (e.g. Americans, Danes have a life expectancy of 77–78 years). So surely it would make sense to tax and subsidize in a way that shifts consumption patterns to the ones seen in countries/regions with the better health results?

Radical problems (a million preventable deaths from heart disease per year in the U.S. alone, etc) require radical solutions. The *hoi polloi* [common people] will be treated to an intense national information campaign informing them of the benefits of the low-fat diet. . . .

Seriously though. The elite has a vested interest in improving the health of the workforce. Firstly, there will appear articles in newspapers and programs on TV exploring the links between nutrition and health. Advocacy groups for healthy dieting will appear, and momentum for legislative changes will build up. Eventually, the government will bow to the public interest and gradually step up the fat tax.

You can still stuff yourself with butter and high-fat cheese if you really want to, you'll just have to pay more for it.

Fast Food Industry Must Change

In industrialized countries, agriculture tends to account for a low % of GDP [gross domestic product] (7.9% in Portugal, 4.6% in Russia, 2.0% in France, 0.9% in the US) and accounts for a correspondingly low % of those countries' workforces (10.0% in Portugal, 10.8% in Russia, 4.1% in France, 0.4% in the US). So a dip in these figures will not affect the national economy much. In any case producers can adjust to it if plenty of advance warning is given and changes are introduced gradually.

Same goes for the food industry. The demand for food will remain; they will just have to try to adjust to the new order of things. Maybe it will be too hard for companies like McDonalds or KFC, but who cares about them anyway?

For some products you can pay very dearly indeed for consuming them (e.g. illegal drugs), i.e. with jail time. Secondly . . . in France and some US states unhealthy snack foods like chips and soft drinks are already subject to taxes.

Currently, even people who would otherwise want to eat healthily are discouraged from doing so because of higher prices, because this is a niche market squeezed by the mainstream food market which is high in fat and sodium.

Incidentally, however, I have always supported legalizing all drugs, for the usual health, monetary and battling hypocrisy reasons, although they would remain heavily taxed (except red wine and to a lesser extent white wine, the consumption of which will be encouraged in moderate daily doses). On the topic of which, fat is actually also a drug—it is both debilitating and makes you irritable and mentally sluggish if consumed to excess in one session.

Finally, consumption of high-fat foods will not, of course, be banned outright. You can still stuff yourself with butter and high-fat cheese if you really want to, you'll just have to pay more for it.

Consumption Patterns Will Change

Today, there is an illogical situation in which rich cakes sometimes cost substantially less than an equivalent weight in fruit or salad, in supermarkets or in catering. The fat tax will reverse this state of affairs by encouraging people to switch consumption patterns to a lower fat, healthier diet. After all, elasticity is high *within* foods.

Currently, even people who would otherwise want to eat healthily are discouraged from doing so because of higher prices, because this is a niche market squeezed by the mainstream food market which is high in fat and sodium.

Yes, it will affect the poor more than the rich. However, consider also the fact that it is the poor who suffer most from low-quality diets and the attendant symptoms of obesity, heart disease, etc. Money from the fat tax can be used to support subsidies to healthy foods, community sports programs and a system of preventative healthcare, all of which are sorely lacking in Russia and the industrialized West.

A fat tax is a profoundly pro-poor measure.

A Market-Based Solution

I have considered converting the food industry into a totally planned thing, on the Soviet model but focused on the goal of fat reduction. Inefficiencies will invariably develop; but since . . . a) [food production] constitutes a fairly small portion of GDP; b) the goals of what to increase, what prices to set, are quite clear; and c) there aren't many food products (relative to advanced industrial goods), it is a sound proposal.

Nonetheless, I think the market-based solution (fat tax, but free setting of prices) should first be completely explored and the planned model considered only if the former fails in its objectives (say, reduce by 50%+ annual cases of heart disease mortality, etc, over a decade since its full implementation). . . .

[Personally,] I have cut out all butter, margarine, vegetable oils (switching to things like balsamic vinegar, salsa and low-fat, low-sodium tomato sauce and Bolognese); cut out jams with any added sugars (there are some preserved with fruit concentrate, which I think is OK); only consume skimmed milk, low-fat cheese; no chocolate or coffee; a glass of red wine per day; only do skinless chicken breast or fish; cut out egg yolks. Of course, I don't always follow it, but the only exceptions are in social settings where I go to a party or gathering, etc. As long as interruptions are infrequent rather than systematic, all is good.

Chicken and fish can be greatly enhanced by tossing in lemon, peppers, all kinds of spices, etc, and served with rice, pasta, etc. . . . For instance, you can even make a delicious carrot cake (calories 159, cholesterol 0, fat 0.6g, *calories from fat 3%*).

The point is that a low-fat diet is only a little bit more restrictive than an unrestricted fat diet, if you bother to find/adapt the appropriate recipes, and it is orders of magnitude better for health/wellbeing. . . .

The key point [of the Fat Tax] is not increased longevity, which due to the high standards of treatment-based modern medical care, is not going to be much more than 5 years or so. The key point is a much increased healthy life expectancy. . . .

Note how in the UK life expectancy has increased much more rapidly than healthy life expectancy. The main trend in this period? More consumption of fats, especially saturated, in the forms of fast food, which has increased obesity levels significantly over this period.

So the question isn't whether you'd like a few more years or not, but whether or not you want to spend the last few years of your life incapacitated and hooked up to mediciny machines.

At least so far. If medical progress continues and radical life extension therapies become available by the middle of this century, those few added years could make the difference between death and immortality!

9

Obese People Should Be Left Alone

Minette Martin

Minette Martin is a London Times *staff writer.*

Obesity is a social class problem generally affecting people with a low income and little education. Lawmakers would like to implement programs to empower people to lose weight and engage in a healthy lifestyle because such programs are likely to curb rapidly escalating healthcare costs. However, it is also possible that obese people have a negligible effect on long-term health costs because their life expectancy tends to be shorter than that of fit people. The government should just leave obese people alone and not interfere with their unhealthy lifestyle choices.

Fat is not a feminist issue, despite what feminists used to say. It is a class issue. Well-to-do, well educated people are rarely fat, still less obese. You see few fat children in private schools. Fatness and obesity are directly related to low income and low education.

A fat map [of Great Britain] was published last week [August, 2008] by Dr Foster Intelligence, showing the areas with the fattest populations, and sure enough the poorest industrial areas in the north of England and in Wales produce the most obese people. The problem seems to be getting worse, fast.

A Class Issue

You hardly need expert medical data analysis to understand that. You need only to go to a few supermarkets. At a Tesco in

Minette Martin, "Leave the Fat Alone—State Bullying Won't Curb Obesity," *TimesOnline*, August 31, 2008. Reproduced by permission of News International Syndication (NI Syndication).

western Scotland this summer I was astonished by the number of horribly obese shoppers waddling round the aisles with their elephantine children, who could not possibly have squashed themselves into an ordinary one-person chair. Young women, with eyes reduced to slits by the pressure of the fat on their faces, laughed grimly with each other as they scanned the shelves. And this is a rich country.

Even though the vast Oban Tesco is full of good food, the trolleys [shopping carts] at the checkout were heaped with stuff that is either useless or positively bad to eat—crisps, snacks, swizzlers, twizzlers and guzzlers, cheesy dips and fatty whatsits, cakes puddings and pies, heavily dusted in additives. The obese seem to fill their carts regularly with several times their own weight in eatables that can make them only fatter, that they shouldn't eat and that nobody should produce, as if they were determined to lay down yet more adipose tissue. Yet you rarely see such bloated people and trolleys in smart supermarkets in rich areas. These days you can easily tell people's precise socioeconomic bracket and body weight by the contents of their trolleys.

Obesity seems to be the issue of the day, possibly because we are still in the silly season. Coincidentally last week, Andrew Lansley, the Tory health spokesman, spoke against obesity in a long speech to the Reform think tank. He was widely understood as saying that fatties have only themselves to blame; they must take responsibility for themselves and their weight because "we all have a choice". And while that is a slightly unfair take on his speech, he does seem to mean something of the sort. Yet at the same time he offers what's now called a whole raft of measures to stop people getting fat. This is awkward for Conservatives; either you interfere with people's choices or you don't. Empowerment, a word he used, is often just a weasel word for state intervention.

State Intervention Is Looming

The question is why a Conservative government should interfere at all in people's inalienable freedom to choke on deep-fried Mars bars if they choose to. The argument is that the fat and the obese (people with a body mass index over 30, which is something you could spot without a calculator) cost the country squillions in lost productivity and increased National Health Service costs. The obese tend to develop serious illness, particularly heart disease and diabetes, and are, generally speaking, crocked up and expensive to look after.

Somebody somewhere has come up with a figure for the cost of all this, which Lansley quotes—£7 billion a year, for what it's worth. Last years Foresight report said this cost could go up by six times by 2050. And fat is getting fatter so fast. According to NHS [National Health Service] figures, the proportion of obese men in the population rose during Labour's time in office from 13.2% in 1993 to 23.1% in 2005. Among women it was even worse, from 16.4% to 24.8%. That is nearly a quarter of all women. If you consider people who are not obese but overweight (with a BMI of 25–30), 46% of men in England are overweight and 32% of women.

If the only reason for interfering with what fat people eat is how much it costs the rest of us, perhaps we should leave them alone.

Fat is also an ethnic issue. According to NHS figures published in 2006, Irish and black Caribbean men had the highest incidence of obesity (25% each) and among women black Africans had 38%, black Caribbean 32% and Pakistani 28%. So, with migration trends and immigrant fertility, the costs of obesity are going to rise fast as well.

Health Costs

However, I wonder how much, if anyone knew the facts, the final cost of obesity would be to the taxpayer. For fat people die sooner and obese people die much sooner than others, thus relieving the NHS and the economy of their needs. It's true that obese people need expensive treatment for diabetes and heart disease before they die, but that might easily be off-set if they had significantly shorter lives—and they do. Current thinking seems to be that the obese die between five and seven years earlier than otherwise they would.

Few papers I've looked at on this subject discuss the possible cost-benefit of obesity, although one from an insurance company coyly mentioned the advantage to pension providers if a person died before he reached pensionable age. For years I used to argue that smokers were a net benefit, purely financially speaking, to the exchequer, because they died early. I still feel rather proud of being the first, I believe, to get a known expert (Professor Richard Peto in 1993) to agree publicly to this idea, now accepted. Might not the same be true of obesity? The real drain on the NHS is geriatric medicine; the obese might not reach old age.

If the only reason for interfering with what fat people eat is how much it costs the rest of us, perhaps we should leave them alone. It's well known that obesity (and fatness) are associated with poor education, poor housing, poor employment or none, low expectations, low opportunities and all the rest. These are all social ills that this government has been trying to deal with for more than a decade. Yet little has improved and obesity—as an indicator of that fact—has swollen vastly while Labour has been in office. What prevents obesity is a good income, a good education, good opportunities and the kind of background that develops self-confidence. Prosperity, in short.

Obesity cannot be defeated by taskforces, better labelling on packets or investing in health accreditation schemes. This has all been tried and has failed. In the presence of a complex problem, and in the absence of a workable solution, perhaps it is better to leave people to their own devices. Nobody can pretend they don't know what they're doing. They should be left alone to do it.

10

Some Forms of Obesity Could Be Designated as a Disability

Greg Cain

Greg Cain is an employment attorney for the New Zealand-based law firm Minter Ellison Rudd Watts.

Obesity is not always caused by a poor diet and a sedentary lifestyle. Biological, behavioral, and environmental factors that a person cannot control may also contribute to his or her obesity. Often, overweight people face discrimination in the workplace when employers and coworkers unfairly believe that their physical appearance will have a detrimental effect on job performance. The courts should consider the possibility of treating obesity like a disability in order to protect overweight people from discrimination.

There was recently some publicity about the decision of the UK Employment Tribunal that a bald teacher, who was subjected to taunts by his pupils, was not disabled, and could not therefore bring a disability discrimination claim.

Okay, fair enough—most of us would not regard baldness as a disability. Lots of other things are, but not (you would have thought) baldness.

But what about obesity? A recent Ministry of Health survey was picked up in the media, partly because it showed that as many as 27% of New Zealanders are obese, and more than a third of us are overweight. The rate of increase is slowing,

Greg Cain, "Could Obesity Be Treated as a Disability?" *New Zealand Herald*, June 25, 2008. Reproduced by permission.

but it's still significantly higher than in 1997, when according to media reports, it was 17% for men and 21% for women.

You don't have to be svelte to be able to analyse legislation, talk to clients or put your case in court.

Obesity Can Have Many Causes

A few years ago, most people would have laughed you out of court for even suggesting that obesity could or should be regarded as a disability. The general attitude towards obese people was (and to an extent still is) that they are fat simply because they eat too much and are too lazy to exercise.

In reality, obesity results from a complex mix of biological, behavioural and environmental factors, and it is rarely as simple as saying, "it's their fault they're so fat". Perhaps more importantly as far as employment is concerned, whether someone is overweight has, or should have, no bearing on a wide range of jobs.

There are some jobs where being obese may fairly disqualify you, such as professional athlete. Even then, being "big" is an advantage in some sports. Many weightlifters, for instance, are of ample proportions. There may also be jobs which obese people could do, but only at significant cost to the employer in terms of special equipment or other support.

But for most jobs, being fat just isn't relevant. Take the practice of law. You don't have to be svelte to be able to analyse legislation, talk to clients or put your case in court. The same goes for a myriad of other jobs. And yet we all know that being fat is frowned upon by many. It's a bit like smoking—it can put you at a disadvantage socially if you're seen to be too big.

The Obese Face Discrimination

In the employment setting, overweight people may face bias from several sources. The U.S. Obesity Society reports that studies have found that when a resume is accompanied by a picture of an overweight person (compared to an "average" weight person), the overweight applicant is rated more negatively and is less likely to be hired.

Other research shows that overweight employees are perceived as lazy, sloppy, less competent, lacking in self-discipline, disagreeable, less conscientious, and poor role models. In addition, overweight employees may suffer financially, as they tend to be paid less for the same jobs, are more likely to have lower paying jobs, and are less likely to get promoted than "normal" people with the same qualifications.

In the U.S., obesity is increasingly the subject of disability discrimination claims.

So, how can society address this problem? Or should it? Attitudes tend to change over time, and views that are regarded as normal by one generation can be seen as backward by the next.

However, often the law has a part to play in changing attitudes—for instance, there is no doubt that the legalisation of sex between gay men in 1986 helped to change social attitudes to homosexuality. Perhaps changing the law to add obesity as a ground of unlawful discrimination is an option.

A more cautious approach would be to leave it to the courts. After all, obesity could in some cases be a disability, which of course is already covered by the discrimination legislation. In the U.S., obesity is increasingly the subject of disability discrimination claims.

U.S. lawyers Tydings and Rosenberg LLP report that although courts initially were reluctant to recognise obesity as a disability, that is changing.

Courts Should Discuss Obesity

The Federal Court has accepted that morbid obesity can be a disability, particularly if caused by a physiological disorder. A Pennsylvania court awarded damages to a fired employee when he was able to show that his former manager had made derogatory comments about his weight. And a Texas decision found that a bus company had improperly decided not to hire an obese woman as a driver, because the company could not demonstrate that her obesity would prevent her from performing the functions of the job.

It remains to be seen whether the courts in New Zealand will take a similar line, or indeed whether there will even be any claims relating to obesity. There is not a significant amount of discrimination litigation here, and a person dismissed or ill-treated purely because of obesity is probably more likely to claim unjustified dismissal or that they were unjustifiably disadvantaged.

Such a claim would likely succeed, unless the employer could show that the person's obesity meant they could not do the job properly. Some jobs may fall into that category, but not many.

11

The Government Should Not Try to Legislate Body Weight

Daniel Hannan

Daniel Hannan is a British politician and Member of the European Parliament (MEP), representing South East England for the Conservative Party. He is also a journalist for the Daily Telegraph.

Despite increasingly alarming calls to address the problem of obesity, there is scant evidence to suggest that society is in the throes of an epidemic. Standards for measuring obesity, most notably the Body Mass Index, only tell part of the story. Indeed, what once was viewed as a sign of a healthy and prosperous lifestyle is now the subject of mass hysteria by a culture obsessed with thinness. Instead of wasting money on government-funded projects to curb obesity, governments should offer assistance only to those who are morbidly overweight.

Yet again, overweight people find themselves surrounded by a baying mob. Force fatties to diet, cry the commentators. Deny them treatment on the NHS [National Health Service]! Make them stop smoking! Put them on treadmills!

This time, the none-too-trim figure of Gordon Brown is leading the bullies. In order to qualify for treatment from his new "personalised" health service, says the PM [Prime Minister], patients might be required to take exercise and lose weight.

Daniel Hannan, "Fat or Thin, It's Not the State's Business," *Daily Telegraph*, February 1, 2008. Telegraph.co.uk. Reproduced by permission.

He knows how to strum a populist chord, Gordon Brown. Fatism is the great acceptable prejudice of our era. It's odd, really: we are generally encouraged to be non-censorious, to refrain from making people feel bad about themselves. But, when it comes to Body Mass Index, we let rip.

A New Form of Discrimination

A few months ago, I wrote a *Telegraph* blog suggesting that much of the obsession with obesity was got up by quangos [quasi non-governmental organization] and interest groups seeking funding.

The blog was immediately deluged with comments of stunning viciousness about the "revolting lard-buckets" whom I was supposedly defending. Oh dear. "For any thing I know, Falstaff shall die of a sweat, unless already he be killed with your hard opinions."

A narrow reading of Body Mass Index . . . defines the entire England rugby squad as obese.

Fatism unites a number of disparate constituencies: anti-Americans who see fat as a U.S. issue; snobs who cling to the last acceptable form of class prejudice; elf-locked anti-globalisation protesters, snatching at another club with which to belabour McDonald's; and, above all, bureaucracies seeking to enlarge their powers.

Whitehall [British government] and, inevitably, Brussels [capital of the European Union] are now bristling with national plans and targets and bans and task-forces, all designed to combat the "obesity epidemic".

(Note the faux-medical language: it is important always to present fatness as an affliction rather than as the result of reasoned choices).

But is the premise correct? Pull out a photograph from a hundred years ago. Observe those jowly Edwardians with their glorious facial hair. See how their paunches strain the fabric of their waistcoats. Are we really that much fatter than they were? Or are we simply vainer?

It's true that, at the extreme edge of the chart, a small number of people are exposing themselves to significantly higher risk from heart disease and diabetes by eating too much.

But most people classified as overweight are in barely any more danger than we thinnies. A narrow reading of Body Mass Index, for example, defines the entire England rugby squad as obese.

Evidence suggests, in any case, that we are sleeker, not just because of dietary changes, but because we now live at constant temperatures, neither sweating off the calories in summer nor shivering them away in winter.

Life-Expectancy Is Still Going Up

After all, if we were truly in the grip of an epidemic, life expectancy would not be stubbornly rising.

Ah, say the anti-fat lobbyists, but the apocalypse is coming. It may not be upon us yet but, unless we mend our ways—unless, in other words, we give more money to the obesity industry—we are heading for calamity.

Sorry, chaps, but I've heard that once too often: CJD [Creutzfeld-Jakob Disease], avian flu—the death toll is always scheduled to take place conveniently in the future.

Don't get me wrong: I'm all in favour of people eating their greens and taking exercise. All I'm saying is that it ought not to be the state's responsibility to keep us in shape.

What Gordon Brown is suggesting would place an almost arbitrary power to withhold treatment in the hands of NHS administrators.

In any other context we should find such a proposal horrifying. But, when it comes to healthcare, we have become so habituated to a 1940s model that denies us contractual rights and treats us as supplicants that we no longer look to ourselves for solutions.

In virtually every other country, there is an element of insurance in healthcare. People who choose to smoke or overeat pay a commensurate premium.

But we British have become so infantilised by the NHS, so drained, demotivated and dependent, that we now accept— no, we now demand—that the Government tells us what to eat.

Government Is Not the Solution

The trouble is that governments do things badly. There is no reason to expect the state to be any better at making us thin than it was at installing telephones, building cars or running airlines. As a rule, bureaucracies become self-sustaining.

Rather than concentrating on the relatively small number of people who are at clinical risk, the obesity lobby, like all lobbies, keeps expanding its remit, constantly talking up the numbers and making people who are only slightly overweight feel bad about themselves.

"There are no respectable reasons for wanting not to be fat," wrote Evelyn Waugh, who knew a thing or two about it. What he meant was most diets, at root, have narcissistic motives.

I can't be the only man who thinks that the skinny models leering at me from magazine covers look unnatural, almost sterile.

The goal of the obesity industry is to conflate the medical concerns about weight to the far more widespread aesthetic ones. These aesthetic objections may be perfectly legitimate; but they are not the proper province of government.

In any case, this constant harping on about porkiness surely carries risks in the other direction. Again, the number of people who place their health at risk through anorexia is relatively small.

But I can't be the only man who thinks that the skinny models leering at me from magazine covers look unnatural, almost sterile.

Nor can I be the only father of little girls who worries that, even if they never come close to developing an eating disorder, their lives will be poorer if they are constantly made anxious about calorific intake.

"Let me have men about me that are fat," says Julius Caesar, "sleek-headed men, and such as sleep o' nights". Shakespeare is, of course, right about almost everything. It ought surely to be possible to be plump, cheerful and at ease with the world.

And it certainly should be acceptable to tuck into whatever you damn well please without being lectured and hectored by government apparatchiks. If sack and sugar be a fault, God help the wicked!

12

Retired Healthcare Professionals Could Help Fight Childhood Obesity

Hugh B. Price and Oliver W. Sloman

Hugh B. Price is a senior fellow at the Brookings Institution. Formerly, he was president and CEO of the National Urban League. He also serves on the board of the Mayo Clinic. Oliver W. Sloman is a senior research assistant at the Brookings Institution.

The best way to combat the obesity epidemic in the United States is to implement early prevention, education, and medical support programs geared at children. However, government and health organizations lack the necessary resources to develop and launch an effective outreach program to reach all of America's communities. One possible solution to this problem is to tap into the large number of physicians and other health care professionals who are retiring or nearly retired. A retired health care professionals corp of volunteers could teach kids how to avoid becoming overweight, help obese children lose weight and adopt a healthier lifestyle, and assist in the management of chronic illnesses related to obesity.

The escalating campaign against childhood obesity gained a resourceful new ally this month when the national YMCA proclaimed that it intends to become America's leading anti-obesity crusader. With their pervasive local presence and their

Hugh B. Price and Oliver W. Sloman, "Mobilizing to Fight Childhood Obesity," Brookings Institute, January 31, 2008. Reproduced by permission.

fitness facilities, YMCA branches will bring many welcome assets to the effort. The challenge now is to link community agencies like the Y, as well as local schools, with health care professionals who can help children and their families ward off obesity and curtail the accompanying chronic illnesses.

Fighting Childhood Obesity

Childhood obesity is one of the most urgent and serious health threats confronting our nation. During the last four decades, obesity rates have soared nearly fivefold among children between the ages of 6 and 11. More than one-third of children and adolescents are overweight or obese. As the Robert Wood Johnson Foundation warns, if our nation fails to reverse this ominous trend, we're in danger of raising the first generation of American children who will live sicker and die younger than the generation before them.

The well-documented culprits include poor diet, insufficient exercise and genetics. Researchers are focusing increasingly on other social and physiological influences that exacerbate these familiar explanations. Evidently the odds of becoming obese are much higher among people with obese friends. One hunch is that those pervasive images of obese hip-hop performers bedecked in "bling" in rap videos reinforce the message to impressionable young people that obesity is cool.

We should deploy vastly more health care professionals . . . to help children and their families cope with and overcome obesity.

Schools Are Serving Healthier Food

Prevention, promotion of healthy lifestyles, and management of chronic disease have been second-class citizens under the health care finance system. The good news is that a survey released last fall by the Centers for Disease Control and Prevention found that the nation's schools have made considerable improvements in nutrition, fitness and health over the last six years. The federal government as well as insurers and employers are beginning to flex their muscle by prodding Medicaid patients and employees to take better care of their health.

These initiatives move us in the right direction. Yet the staggering scale of the epidemic means all-out combat against childhood obesity. We need, in military terms, more boots on the ground. In other words, we should deploy vastly more health care professionals, namely doctors, nurses and nurses' aides, physical fitness specialists and more to help children and their families cope with and overcome obesity.

Our idea is to mobilize retired physicians and health care workers to serve their country by joining in a crusade to combat childhood obesity, especially in those communities and among the children where the problem is most acute. They could serve in schools, YWCAs, Boys and Girls Clubs, community centers, neighborhood clinics, childcare centers, churches and other venues where they can establish and sustain regular contact with children and their families.

Retirees Can Make a Difference

Health care professionals who have retired, or are on the cusp of retiring, constitute a potentially vast resource that could be tapped. According to the National Association of Retired Physicians, 250,000 doctors are age 55 or over. As these baby boomers wind down their practices, many undoubtedly will have the interest, energy and public spiritedness to contribute their time and expertise to a pressing cause like combating childhood obesity.

Several approaches to mobilizing retirees come to mind. One way is to emulate and expand the many local efforts already under way. Another is to call upon states to take the initiative.

There arguably is a more logical, convenient and potentially scalable option. The Corporation for National and Community Service is the independent federal agency created in 1994 to oversee domestic community service programs like AmeriCorps, VISTA [Volunteers in Service to America] and the Senior Corps. The latter connects 500,000 volunteers age 55 and older with people and organizations that need support.

We could create a Retired Health Care Professionals Corps under the aegis of the Senior Corps, with volunteers deployed to keep kids from becoming overweight and obese, to assist helping overweight and obese children to lose weight and adopt healthier lifestyles and to help overweight and obese youngsters manage the chronic illnesses that may develop as a result of their condition.

As with any novel endeavor, a number of thorny issues must be addressed and resolved. For instance, besides tapping pediatricians and family practitioners, could a former cardiologist be of service? Would volunteers be obliged to carry malpractice insurance? And, to what extent could these physician-volunteers function from home?

A careful feasibility analysis to answer these questions is a logical next step. Aligning an underutilized asset with an urgent societal need, the Retired Health Care Professional Corps could prove to be an invaluable weapon in America's fight against childhood obesity.

13

Educational Games Can Teach Kids About the Dangers of Obesity

Kathy SaeNgian

Kathy SaeNgian is a double major in journalism and English at Duquesne University. She is also vice president of the Duquesne Chapter of the Society for Professional Journalists.

Rather than relying on the traditional food pyramid to teach children about proper nutrition, educators have developed an unconventional and fun program designed to instruct kids about the benefits of exercising and maintaining a healthy diet. Geared toward children between the ages of 9 and 12, the "Fitwits" program features funny, interesting characters on flashcards who explain the positive effects of proper nutrition and the negative effects of unhealthy eating. The characters also appear on trading cards and on a memory game so that the program's educational message is continually reinforced when children play the games with their friends and families.

Teaching children about obesity and how to eat healthfully doesn't always have to be a drag.

Instead of the traditional food pyramid, Pittsburgh fifth-graders will learn health awareness through Chunky Hunky and Sunny Yolk, characters in a new health education program designed by Carnegie Mellon University.

"We always learn about the food pyramid in school, but it's boring so we don't remember it," said Azasha Beard, 12, of

Kathy SaeNgian, "Diet of Fun: Fitwits Program Helps Adolescents Fight Obesity," *Post-Gazette Now* (Pittsburgh), August 20, 2008. Reproduced by permission of the author.

East Liberty. Azasha and her sister Elizabeth, 11, were the first adolescents to test the new program at UPMC [University of Pittsburgh Medical Center] St. Margaret Family Health Center in Lawrenceville.

Fitwits is a health education program that targets adolescents between 9 and 12 years old and teaches them how to avoid obesity and other related health complications.

Fighting Childhood Obesity

The program was created as a response to the number of overweight adolescents increasing by more than 8 percent over the past decade, making it one of the leading health concerns in the United States, according to the Centers for Disease Control and Prevention.

"Obesity is a silent disease because nobody wants to talk about it," said Kristin Hughes, associate professor at the Carnegie Mellon University School of Design.

Ms. Hughes and a small team of students and kids created a series of educational tools to help teach adolescents about obesity and how to avoid it.

Nitwits like Fry Girl and Biggie Allbeef show kids what to avoid and how to monitor their portions.

Caren Audenried, 20, and Jung Paek, 23, are undergraduates in the communication design program at Carnegie Mellon University and helped to make the game appropriate for children. They also work with senior Melissa Dolin, 21, of the creative and technical writing and art program.

Before the program launched, Ms. Hughes and her three students held a series of focus groups with 100 youngsters between 9 and 12 from Bloomfield and Garfield. The kids provided insight on the coolest ways to present the information.

Making Health Information Fun

"Medicine has needed designers for a long time to help deliver the information that we already know is important. That is the biggest dilemma," said Dr. Susan Fidler, a resident at UPMC St. Margaret Family Health Center. "This game is all encompassing and helps us deliver the information."

The program presents adolescents with two types of characters: Fitwits and Nitwits. Fitwits like Elvis Pretzley and Queen of Wheat teach kids about obesity and the importance of being active. Nitwits like Fry Girl and Biggie Allbeef show kids what to avoid and how to monitor their portions.

It teaches you how to be healthy without it being really confusing.

The characters will be introduced to fifth-graders in public schools around the city in a one-hour presentation by the end of this year [2008]. At this time, kids will learn about the characters and how they affect their diets.

Then, flash cards will be used in UPMC St. Margaret Family Health Centers to expand upon what the kids already learned in school. The cards teach kids about the appropriate Body Mass Index for boys and girls and how to eat right.

Identifying Obesity

During the program's trial run, Azasha and Elizabeth were asked to define obesity and if anyone in their family was obese. After identifying that their mother was obese, Dr. Ann McGaffey of the health centers explained how the condition causes other health concerns like type 2 diabetes, high blood pressure and heart disease.

The girls also learned how to measure their portions at home by using their hands. Family members should consume only one palm-size portion of meat, a fist full of vegetables and thumb tip worth of butter or dressing at each meal.

"It teaches you how to be healthy without it being really confusing. It is important to know what the right balance is for everyone," said Ms. Hughes. "Every kid who gets the talk will also get the game that the whole family can play together. It's a holistic way to talk about getting healthy."

The team created a memory game for kids to take home. In the game, family members have to answer trivia questions about staying healthy before they can take their turn.

Kids also will be given trading cards that provide background information about each of the Fitwit and Nitwit characters. The trading cards also have fun and easy snack recipes that serve as a healthy alternative to fatty fast food.

All of the components of Fitwits were funded by a $195,000 Heinz Endowments grant, but Ms. Hughes hopes to attain more sponsors to make this a national trend.

"In the future, we would like to get the support of insurance companies so that physicians can get trained to teach simple nutrition to kids," she said.

14

Society and Governments Are Overreacting to the Obesity Problem

Dominic Lawson

Dominic Lawson is a British journalist who writes columns for the Independent *and the* Sunday Times.

Despite sweeping paranoia about an obesity epidemic over-whelming society, physicians have yet to agree upon a measur-able set of criteria to define what obesity is. Indeed, some scien-tific studies that find that people are getting dangerously overweight are sponsored by pharmaceutical companies who have a vested interest in selling weight-loss drugs to a fearful population. In addition, government officials who engage in rhetoric critical of obesity typically do so for political reasons and not out of concern for their constituents' welfare. In the ab-sence of compelling, unbiased scientific evidence about the dan-gers of obesity, the government and society as a whole should leave overweight people alone.

Y ou can run, but you can't hide: a wave of contagious obe-sity is, apparently, sweeping the country from top to (ever-expanding) bottom. Yesterday's *Guardian* declared that "Obe-sity epidemic spreads to new areas in the south", while simultaneously pointing out that "the worst obesity hotspot is Shetland". Meanwhile the *Financial Times* warned, rather in the style of a Meteorological Office alert, of "a belt of obesity stretching across Wales, the north Midlands and northern En-gland".

Dominic Lawson, "Don't Believe Obesity Figures—They're Spun for a Reason," *The In-dependent*, August 29, 2008. Reproduced by permission.

Yes, it's still August, and even the more unsensationalist newspapers are prepared to swallow whole the sort of statistical surveys which would normally end up impaled on the news editor's spike. For both of these stories—and many others, along exactly the same lines—are a regurgitation of a report from an organisation called Dr Foster Research. What some of these supposedly terrifying reports fail to tell us is who paid for this research. It was funded by Roche, the pharmaceutical company which developed the anti-obesity drug Xenical.

This does not in itself discredit the survey—but it's still useful to know what its ultimate purpose might be. A year ago, for example, Dr Foster issued a report which complained that "around 3 per cent of Primary Care Organisations do not fund the use of drug therapy for obesity, despite the recommendations of organisations such as the National Institute for Clinical Excellence." With a crafty eye for the prevailing political wind, this press release from 'Dr Foster' was headlined "New audit reveals inequality in NHS services to tackle obesity across the UK."

More pertinently for us all, there is nothing wrong, or even unhealthy, in being obese, at least as defined by the official measurement known as the Body Mass Index.

That particular "audit" was funded by Abbott Laboratories, developers of the anti-obesity drug Reductil; it was obviously not designed to address the question of whether the 3 per cent of PCOs which chose not to prescribe pharmaceutical treatments for obesity had decided that there were more urgent or deserving causes to be treated by means of their drugs budget, or perhaps simply took the view that these slimming drugs had side effects which could outweigh the benefits.

Dr Foster's latest "audit of obesity" has at least attracted some criticism, following its initially uncritical reproduction by the press and broadcasters. The MSP for Shetland, Tavish Scott, said that it was "absolutely ridiculous to suggest that Shetland is an obesity hotspot". NHS Shetland declared that Dr Foster's audit was based on "flawed research". Well, they would say that: but there does seem to be something fishy in a report which has Glasgow well down the "obesity league" with a figure of 6.6 per cent of the local population, while Shetland comes out worst in the entire country, at 15.5 per cent.

I do have a doctor friend, a great worrier about obesity, who claims that the further north he travels in the United Kingdom, the wider people's bottoms seem to be—especially among the female population, he insists—but even so I can't help feeling that the people of our most northerly outpost do not merit being stigmatised as the tubbiest in the land. And even if they were indeed so well layered, they have a particular requirement for such internal lagging which provides much needed warmth for the inhabitants of a cold and remote spot; they therefore deserve our understanding, rather than our criticism.

More pertinently for us all, there is nothing wrong, or even unhealthy, in being obese, at least as defined by the official measurement known as the Body Mass Index. Admittedly, I speak as a man of average height who weighs 15 stones; but on current BMI definitions George Clooney and Russell Crowe are clinically "obese" while Brad Pitt and Mel Gibson are "overweight". Meanwhile another doctor friend of mine points out that many of his anorexic patients would be classified as very healthy according to most conventional measurements, such as blood pressure; but clearly their attitude to food is anything but healthy.

Do not expect such arguments to weigh heavily with the political class. Both the Government and the official Opposition are engaged in a battle over which of them can appear most productively concerned about "the obesity epidemic". The Conservatives have found it a rewarding way of scoring easy points off a punch-drunk Labour administration. A few weeks ago, David Cameron declared that the Government had failed to stress personal responsibility for obesity: we should stop talking about it as something that just happens to people, he said: they needed to pull their socks up—specifically, to eat less and exercise more. This week, however, the Conservatives seem simultaneously to be taking the completely different tack that it is all part of a growing inequality between the various social classes which it accuses the Government of failing to address.

Anyone who has attempted to persuade their own unwilling child to eat an unwanted salad or vegetable will be instinctively sceptical about the state's ability to succeed in enforcing dietary correctness.

There is, in fact, almost no difference in the rate of so-called "obesity" between people of different income levels. It is possibly true that truly morbid obesity is now more common among the poorer, when once it was the exclusive privilege of the most affluent—Queen Victoria and her son Edward VII both boasted figures which did not deviate much from the spherical. This modern trend, which differentiates the developed world from less fortunate nations, is not a result of increasing relative poverty in the UK, as so many insist: instead it demonstrates that, at least in terms of food purchasing power, we have, after the U.S., the richest poor people in the world.

In any case, what are we supposed to do for those who choose to eat vastly more calories than they burn up through work or exercise? When the Government imposed Jamie Oliver's "school dinners revolution" on the state education system, it backfired almost comically, as increasing numbers of pupils abandoned the newly "healthy" school canteen, while their anxious mothers pushed Big Macs at them through the school railings. Anyone who has attempted to persuade their own unwilling child to eat an unwanted salad or vegetable will be instinctively sceptical about the state's ability to succeed in enforcing dietary correctness.

Even with all the panic partially promoted by the manufacturers of slimming pills, we are at least a long way from emulating the law recently imposed in Japan: this requires all adult citizens to have their waists measured by order of the state, and if they repeatedly exceed the allowable limit—33.5 inches for men and 35.4 inches for women—they are subjected to "health re-education" and their employers become liable to financial penalties.

An overweight nation might indeed be aesthetically less attractive than, say, the Nubian tribes whose physical perfection so transfixed the late Leni Riefenstahl, but we should still treasure the freedom to grow into shapes which reflect our own pleasures, rather than the requirements of conventional wisdom or the box-ticking desire of officialdom for a lower national average waistline.

Organizations to Contact

The editors have compiled the following list of organizations concerned with the issues debated in this book. The descriptions are derived from materials provided by the organizations. All have publications or information available for interested readers. The list was compiled on the date of publication of the present volume; the information provided here may change. Be aware that many organizations take several weeks or longer to respond to inquiries, so allow as much time as possible.

American Dietetic Association (ADA)
216 West Jackson Blvd., Chicago, IL   60606-6995
(800) 877-1600
Web site: www.eatright.org

The American Dietetic Association is the world's largest organization of food and nutrition professionals. ADA seeks to improve the nation's health and advance the profession of dietetics through research, education, and advocacy. Articles, research findings, and the *Journal of the American Dietetic Association* can be accessed online.

The American Society for Metabolic and Bariatric Surgery (ASMBS)
100 SW 75th Street, Suite 201, Gainesville, FL   32607
(352) 331-4900 • Fax: (352) 331-4975
E-mail: info@asmbs.org
Web site: www.asbs.org/html/rationale/rationale.html

ASMBS wants to improve public health and well-being by lessening the burden of the disease of obesity and related diseases throughout the world. American surgeons have formed the society's leadership and have established an organization with educational and support programs for surgeons and integrated health professionals. The purpose of the society is to advance the art and science of bariatric surgery. Articles and information are published on the society's Web site.

American Psychological Association (APA)
750 First Street NE, Washington, DC   20002-4242
(202) 336-5500 • Fax: (202) 336-5708
E-mail: public.affairs@apa.org
Web site: www.apa.org

The APA aims to "advance psychology as a science, as a profession, and as a means of promoting human welfare." It produces numerous publications, including the monthly journal *American Psychologist*, the monthly newspaper *APA Monitor*, and the quarterly *Journal of Abnormal Psychology*.

Centers for Disease Control and Prevention (CDC)
1600 Clifton Road, Atlanta, GA   30333
800-CDC-INFO (800-232-4636)
E-mail: cdcinfo@cdc.gov
Web site: www.cdc.gov

The CDC's mission is to help create the expertise, information, and tools that people and communities need to protect their health—through health promotion; prevention of disease, injury, and disability; and preparedness for new health threats. Articles and fact sheets are provided online.

KidsHealth
Web site: www.KidsHealth.org

Created by The Nemours Foundation's Center for Children's Health Media, TeensHealth and KidsHealth provide teens and families with accurate, up-to-date, and jargon-free health information. Medical experts post fact sheets on their Web site for children, teens, and parents covering obesity, body mass index, eating disorders, activity patterns for children and teens, and other topics.

National Eating Disorders Association (NEDA)
603 Stewart Street, Suite 803, Seattle, WA   98101
(206) 382-3587 • Fax: (206) 292-9890
Web site: www.nationaleatingdisorders.org

NEDA promotes the awareness and prevention of eating disorders by encouraging self-esteem. It provides free and low-cost educational information on eating disorders and their prevention. NEDA also provides educational outreach programs and training for schools and universities.

The Obesity Society
8630 Fenton Street, Suite 814, Silver Spring, MD   20910
(301) 563-6526 • Fax: (301) 563-6595
Web site: www.obesity.org

The Obesity Society is committed to encouraging research on the causes and treatment of obesity, and to keeping the medical community and public informed of new advances. It seeks to improve the lives of those with obesity, nurture careers of obesity scientists and practitioners, and promote the interdisciplinary nature of obesity research, management, and education. The Obesity Society's official journal, *Obesity*, publishes original scientific articles, as well as relevant review articles, commentaries, and public health and medical news.

Shape Up America!
6707 Democracy Blvd., Bethesda, MD   20817
Web site: www.shapeup.org/index.php

The purpose of Shape Up America! is to educate the public on the importance of the achievement and maintenance of a healthy body weight through the adoption of increased physical activity and healthy eating. By clearly defining obesity as a major public health issue, Shape Up America! is conducting a broad-based education initiative to encourage sensible eating and increased physical activity in all individuals and a modest weight loss in overweight individuals that can be maintained over time. Information about obesity and healthy diets is published on their Web site.

Weight-Control Information Network (WIN)
1 WIN Way, Bethesda, MD   20892-3665
(877) 946-4627
Web site: www.niddk.nih.gov/health/nutrit/nutrit.htm

This division of the U.S. National Institute for Diabetes and Digestive and Kidney Diseases (NIDDK) provides information about obesity, weight control, nutrition, weight-loss medications, and gastric surgery. Articles and reports are available online.

Bibliography

Books

American Psychiatric Association	*Diagnostic and Statistical Manual of Mental Disorders*, 4th edition, Washington, DC: American Psychiatric Association, 2000.
Rolf Benirschke	*Great Comebacks from Ostomy Surgery*, Rancho Santa Fe, CA: Rolf Benirschke Enterprises Inc., 2002.
Michelle Boasten	*Weight Loss Surgery: Understanding and Overcoming Morbid Obesity*, Akron, OH: FBE Service Network & Network Publishing, 2002.
Jana Evans Braziel and Kathleen Le Besco	*Bodies out of Bounds: Fatness and Transgression*, Berkeley: University of California Press, 2001.
Kelly Brownell, Rebecca Puhl, Marlene Schwartz, and Leslie Rudd	*Weight Bias: Nature, Consequences, and Remedies*, New York: Guilford Press, 2005.
Walter Burniat, Tim Cole, Inge Lissau, and Elizabeth Poskitt	*Child and Adolescent Obesity: Causes and Consequences, Prevention and Management*, Cambridge, UK: Cambridge University Press, 2002.

Sharron Dalton — *Our Overweight Children: What Parents, Schools, and Communities Can Do to Control the Fatness Epidemic*, Berkeley: University of California Press, 2004.

John Evans, Brian Davies, and Jan Wright — *Body Knowledge and Control: Studies in the Sociology of Physical Education and Health*, New York: Routledge, 2004.

Christopher Fairburn and Kelly Brownell — *Eating Disorders and Obesity: A Comprehensive Handbook*, New York: Guilford Press, 2002.

Louis Flancbaum — *The Doctor's Guide to Weight Loss Surgery*, New York: Bantam Doubleday Dell, 2003.

Michael Gard and Jan Wright — *The Obesity Epidemic: Science, Morality, and Ideology*, New York: Routledge, 2004.

Adrianne Hardman and David Stensel — *Physical Activity and Health: The Evidence Explained*, New York: Routledge, 2003.

Wieland Kiess, Claude Marcus, and Martin Wabitsch, eds. — *Obesity in Childhood and Adolescence*, Basel, Switzerland: S. Karger AG, 2004.

Gina Kolata — *Rethinking Thin: The New Science of Weight Loss—and the Myths and Realities of Dieting*, New York: Picador, 2007.

Peter Kopelman   *The Management of Obesity and Related Disorders*, London: Martin Dunitz, 2001.

Mark Lawrence and Tony Worsley   *Public Health Nutrition: From Principles to Practice*, Australia: Allen & Unwin, 2007.

Kathy Leach   *The Overweight Patient: A Psychological Approach to Understanding and Working with Obesity*, London: Jessica Kingsley, 2006.

Alexandra Logue   *The Psychology of Eating and Drinking*, New York: Brunner-Routledge, 2004.

Robert Pool   *Fat: Fighting the Obesity Epidemic*, Oxford: Oxford University Press, 2001.

B. Thompson   *Weight Loss Surgery: Finding the Thin Person Hiding Inside You*, Tarentum, PA: Word Association Publishers, 2002.

Janet Treasure, Ulrike Schmidt, and Eric Van Furth   *Handbook of Eating Disorders*, Malden, MA: John Wiley & Sons, 2003.

U.S. Department of Health and Human Services   *The Surgeon General's Call to Action to Prevent and Decrease Overweight and Obesity*, Rockville, MD: U.S. Department of Health and Human Services, Public Health Service, Office of the Surgeon General, 2001.

Bryan Woodward   *A Complete Guide to Obesity Surgery: Everything You Need to Know About Weight Loss Surgery and How to Succeed*, New Bern, NC: Trafford Publishing, 2001.

World Health Organization   *Obesity: Preventing and Managing the Global Epidemic*, Geneva: World Health Organization, 2000.

Periodicals

Osama Al-Saif, et al.   "Who Should Be Doing Laparoscopic Bariatric Surgery?" *Obesity Surgery*, February 13, 2003.

Glenn Cardwell   "Legislating Obesity Through Food Taxes?" *Manufacturing Confectioner*, 2002.

Council on Sports Medicine and Fitness and Council on School Health   "Active Healthy Living: Prevention of Childhood Obesity Through Increased Physical Activity," *Pediatrics*, 2006.

Laura Fraser   "Body Love, Body Hate," *Glamour*, October 2002.

Dave Fusaro   "Misplaced Blame and Ignorance," *Food Processing*, January 2006.

Denise Grady   "Seeking to Shed Fat, She Lost Her Liver," *New York Times*, March 4, 2003.

Michael Jensen, ed.   "Obesity," *Medical Clinics of North America*, March 2000.

Jean Kinsey — "Whole Health for Self-Care—A New Nutrition," *Cereal Foods World*, 2002.

Jeffrey Koplan, Catharyn Liverman, and Vivica Kraak — "Preventing Childhood Obesity: The Nation Must Act Now, or It Will Watch Its Children Grow into Adults with Excessive Levels of Diabetes, Heart Disease, Cancer, and Other Weight-Related Ailments," *Issues in Science and Technology*, Spring 2005.

Mianna Lotz — "Childhood Obesity and the Question of Parental Liberty," *Journal of Social Philosophy*, 2004.

Lisa Mancino — "Americans at Unequal Risk for Obesity," *Amber Waves*, November 2004.

Betsy McKay — "Obesity Epidemic May Not Be As Deadly As Claimed," *Wall Street Journal*, April 30, 2005.

Marcia Menter — "Why Don't Magazines Show Clothes On More Real-Size Women?" *Glamour*, November 2001.

Manesh Patel and Darren McGuire — "Pounds of Prevention," *American Heart Journal*, September 2001.

Emma Patterson, et al. — "A Comparison of Diet and Exercise Therapy versus Laparoscopic Roux-en-Y Gastric Bypass Surgery for Morbid Obesity: A Decision Analysis Model," *Journal of the American College of Surgeons*, March 2003.

Michele Ploeg, Lisa Mancino, and Biing-Hwan Lin	"Food Stamps and Obesity: Ironic Twist or Complex Puzzle?" *Amber Waves*, February 2006.
Walker Poston and John Foreyt	"Body Mass Index: Uses and Limitations," *Strength and Conditioning Journal*, 2002.
Sowsan Rasheid, et al.	"Gastric Bypass Is an Effective Treatment for Obstructive Sleep Apnea in Patients with Clinically Significant Obesity," *Obesity Surgery*, February 13, 2003.
Alan Robinson	"Starstruck," *Frozen Food Age*, November 2006.
Albert Rocchini	"Childhood Obesity and a Diabetes Epidemic," *New England Journal of Medicine*, March 14, 2002.
Sylvia Rowe	"The Obesity Epidemic: A Complex Problem with No Simple Solution," *Manufacturing Confectioner*, 2002.
John Spizzirri	"Weighing Weight-Management Options," *Food Product Design*, January 2006.
Ala Stanford, et al.	"Laparoscopic Roux-en-Y Gastric Bypass in Morbidly Obese Adolescents," *Journal of Pediatric Surgery*, March 2003.
John Stanton	"Obesity: Take the Offensive," *Food Processing*, January 2005.

Marcia Wood, Jan Suszkiw, Jim Core, and Erin Peabody   "Cooking Up Tempting, Fat-Fighting Foods and Ingredients," *Agricultural Research*, March 2006.

Rachel Zimmerman,   "Obesity May Shrink U.S. Lifespan," *Wall Street Journal*, March 17, 2005.

Index